THE
Quinceañera
HANDBOOK

THE ULTIMATE GUIDE TO PLANNING,
ORGANIZING, AND CELEBRATING
YOUR BIG DAY LIKE A BOSS

ISA MARTINEZ

Oh
HAPPY
DAY
PRESS

Contents

Introduction   1

1. Evolving Traditions   5

2. Your Dream Team   9

3. From Ceremony to Reception   19

4. Develop Your Vision   29

5. Budget Like a Pro   41

6. Manage Like a Boss   51

7. Find the Perfect Location   69

8. Guest Lists & Communication   79

9. Menu Planning   91

10. Dresses & Attire   101

11. Hair, Makeup, & Self-Care   117

12. Music & Dance   129

13. Speeches & Toasts   139

14. Document & Share   145

15. Post-Event Tasks & Reflections   157

16. The Next Chapter   161

Introduction

Your quinceañera is a day of celebration, joy, and love, surrounded by your nearest and dearest friends and family. The day marks a major milestone in your life and is a symbol of your transition from childhood to young adulthood.

On the day of your quinceañera, you feel excitement and anticipation, as well as a sense of pride and accomplishment. Every detail of your quinceañera has been carefully planned to make this day special, and the many moments that make up the event will be forever etched in your memory. It's truly a joyous occasion, filled with traditions and customs that reflect your rich culture and heritage.

As you celebrate this important milestone in your life, I'm honored to be here to guide you through it. I've always been inspired by the beauty and significance of this celebration, and touched by the outpouring of love from friends and family. Throughout the pages of this book, you'll find practical advice, guidance, and inspiration to help you with everything, from choosing the perfect dress to creating a memorable ceremony and reception.

Whether you're planning a traditional quinceañera, or putting your own spin on this tradition, I'm here to coach you every step of the way and help make your special day truly unforgettable.

I also know that planning a quinceañera can be a daunting experience. From the ceremony to the guest list to the venue, menu, music, and more, it's easy to get lost in the details and lose sight of what's really important: celebrating you in the company of your favorite people!

Add to that juggling school, a social life, and other commitments, and it's completely normal to feel stressed out. But don't worry, with a few helpful tips and tricks, you can turn your quinceañera dreams into reality and have fun doing it too!

In my years as an event planner, I've helped families create cherished memories, from backyard barbecues to debutante balls. I've also produced large corporate events with thousands of guests. I'm excited to share my knowledge and experiences with you as you plan your special day so that you can enjoy the process more and stress less while planning the event of your life!

There's another reason I decided to write this book: I'm passionate about empowering girls to feel confident in taking on responsibilities and challenges and setting them up for success. I believe a quinceañera presents a wonderful opportunity for you to gain valuable life skills in planning your special day. You'll be making decisions and taking on challenges that require you to juggle responsibilities with finesse. After all, this celebration symbolizes the transition from childhood to adulthood. I know you can do this!

I'll take you through each step of the process, from developing your vision to finding the perfect venue to selecting music for your dances. You'll practice skills like research, decision-making, communication, collaboration, negotiation, delegation, budgeting, and more, that will serve you well in the future and in just about anything you decide to pursue.

Whether you're a quinceañera, a family member, a friend, or an event planner, this book has something for you. With practical tips and suggestions that cover every aspect of the celebration, from the ceremony to the reception, you'll have the tools you need to make this the event of your dreams.

Thank you so much for letting me be a part of your special day. I know you are on your way to creating a beautiful and memorable celebration, one that reflects the amazing young woman you are to become, and that you will cherish forever!

You've got this, girl! Congratulations on your quinceañera, and let's get started!

CHAPTER ONE

Evolving Traditions

QUINCEAÑERAS ARE AN IMPORTANT celebration and milestone in the Latin American community, representing a girl's transition into a young woman and her presentation to society. It has a long cultural history, with traditions that have evolved and been influenced by various societies and religions over centuries. From ancient civilizations to colonialism, and religious rites to cultural celebrations, the history of the quinceañera is a complex tapestry woven together by many different threads.

In recent times, the celebration has been further influenced by a blending of modern customs and cultures. Yet, the essence of the quinceañera remains the same: a celebration of a girl's transition into womanhood, with family and friends coming together to honor her and the journey ahead.

The history of the quinceañera dates back to ancient civilizations. In pre-Columbian times, the Aztecs and Mayans held ceremonies to mark a girl's transition into womanhood, which included dancing and feasting. These celebrations often included religious rituals and offerings to the gods.

Over time, these indigenous cultures combined with European traditions, where similar customs existed, particularly in Spain and

France. The quinceañera's roots in Catholicism were originally seen as a way to mark a girl's marriageability, with gifts and dresses intended for her dowry. However, today, the meaning has evolved to focus more on the transition from childhood to adolescence, and the celebration of a young woman's growth and accomplishments.

While quinceañeras are widely celebrated across Latin America, each country adds its own unique touches to the festivities. As Latin communities from various countries come together, different traditions and customs are often combined or adapted to create a unique celebration that reflects the diversity and rich heritage of the attendees.

Today, the modern quinceañera tradition is strongest in Mexico, where it is said to have originated during the viceregal or Mexican imperial periods. There, the celebration often includes a special mass at church. In the Dominican Republic, it's common for the birthday girl to wear a brightly colored gown, while in Ecuador, quinceañeras are often referred to as *fiesta rosada* or "pink party" due to the abundance of pink decorations and attire. In Brazil, a Portuguese-speaking country, a comparable celebration is called *festa de debutantes*, *baile de debutantes*, or *festa de quinze anos*. In the French Caribbean and French Guyana, it is known as *fête des quinze ans*.

Despite these differences, there are common elements that unite quinceañeras across cultures. It is generally accepted that quinceañeras mark a girl's 15th birthday and her transition into a more mature phase of life. These celebrations typically include a religious ceremony, such as a Catholic mass, family and friends, the celebrant in a formal gown, and symbolic customs like the changing of the shoes and the last doll. A court of honor often accompanies the quinceañera, and the event is filled with food, music, and dancing.

Quinceañeras in the United States have also evolved to reflect the cultural landscape of the country. The most extravagant parties resemble debutante balls and are often influenced by modern American culture. It is not uncommon to find quinceañeras with themes inspired by Hollywood, or popular American books, movies, and culture. The incorporation of non-traditional colors, music, and dress styles can also be seen as a result of this fusion.

The influence of American culture has also led some families to opt for a more relaxed or informal celebration, while still maintaining the essence and significance of the quinceañera. This has also encouraged a greater emphasis on individuality, allowing the young woman to showcase her personality and style throughout the event.

Families sometimes choose to forgo the church ceremony or big party altogether. Some families prefer a small, intimate celebration at home, while others might offer their daughters a birthday cruise with friends, a trip abroad, a monetary gift, or a car.

One growing trend is the destination quinceañera. Havana, Cuba, is an increasingly popular destination that includes photoshoots featuring colorful vintage cars and picturesque backgrounds. In recent years, some women have opted for a "double quince" celebrating a milestone at 30 instead of 15. This modern twist on the traditional quinceañera allows women to redefine the celebration in a way that resonates with them personally.

As quinceañeras continue to be celebrated in the United States, Latin America, Mexico, and the Caribbean, they will likely continue to evolve and adapt to the changing cultural landscape.

No matter how you choose to celebrate, quinceañeras represent a rich history and a profound connection to culture, family, and community. As you prepare for your own quinceañera, remember that this special day is a once-in-a-lifetime opportunity to honor your heritage, embrace your unique identity, and celebrate with the people who love and support you the most.

CHAPTER TWO
Your Dream Team

WITH SO MANY DECISIONS to make and tasks to complete, one of the first things you'll need to do is assemble a core team. This team includes your court of honor, family members, madrinas, and padrinos, who will provide guidance, and support, and share the spotlight with you on your big day.

In addition to your core team, you might also have an extended team of officiants, professionals, and vendors who will also contribute greatly to the success of your celebration. Your core team and extended team make up your dream team and ensure that your quinceañera goes off according to plan and is as magical as you envisioned.

The Court of Honor (*Corte de Honor*)

Selecting your court of honor is one of the most exciting and important parts of planning your quinceañera. These are the special people in your life who have been there for you, supporting and encouraging you along the way.

Your court is made up of close family members and friends

who will stand by your side and participate in dances and special moments throughout the celebration.

When selecting your quinceañera court members, think about the people who have played a significant role in your life. This can include siblings, cousins, close friends, or even classmates. Your quince court should be made up of people who genuinely care about you and are excited to support and celebrate with you on your big day.

- **Chambelanes**: Chambelanes (also known as *chamberlains*) are the male members of your court who escort you during the celebration. They typically dress in formal attire. During the celebration, they participate in dances and activities, and may also assist in other aspects of the celebration, such as coordinating with the DJ or helping with decorations.

- **Chambelan of Honor (*Chambelan de Honor*)**: This is someone you have a close relationship with — they could be a brother, cousin, or a close friend. The Chambelan de Honor's job is to be your escort throughout the evening. The role is both ceremonial and practical. In addition to accompanying you during your grand entrance, and taking part in the special dances, they may also assist with tasks such as carrying your purse and helping you navigate the reception in your dress.

- **Damas**: These are the girls and young women you choose to be a part of your court. They typically wear matching dresses and will dance with the chambelanes during the celebration. The damas play an important role in supporting you and adding to the overall beauty and elegance of the event.

Court Size

The size of your quinceañera court can vary depending on personal preferences and the scale of your celebration. Traditionally, a quinceañera has 14 damas and 14 chambelanes to represent each year of your life leading up to your 15th birthday. However, you can choose to have a smaller or larger court or even an all-girl or all-boy court.

A half court of 7 damas and 7 chambelanes is a popular choice as there are still 14 members to represent each year of the quinceañera's life but the reduced number makes it easier to organize and is more cost-effective. Another configuration is to have a court of 7 damas, with each girl escorted by a male relative. It's really up to you and your family to decide what works best for your quinceañera.

Commitment

Being a part of a quince court comes with responsibilities. Your court will need to attend rehearsals, help with planning, and be present at your celebration. Make sure your chosen friends and family members are enthusiastic and committed to participating in your quinceañera. It will require time and possibly even financial commitment, so be sure that they are aware of what you are asking of them and that they have agreed to it.

Appreciation

Your quinceañera court is an essential part of your celebration, so be sure to show your appreciation for their support and involvement. Serve food at the rehearsals. It can be as simple as chips or takeout, but keep your squad fed and happy. Consider giving them a small token of appreciation before the event, like matching t-shirts, makeup bags, or keychains. Even a simple, sincere thank you is enough to generate goodwill.

Family, Madrinas, & Padrinos

Your core team consists of your court, but of equal importance is your support system made up of your family and loved ones. This might include your mother, father, madrinas (godmothers), padrinos (godfathers), family members, and other people who mean something to you.

You may choose to have a Madrina de Honor and/or a Padrino de Honor. These individuals are an integral part of your quinceañera journey, providing emotional, financial, and logistical support throughout the planning process and on your big day.

Your madrinas and padrinos might sponsor specific aspects of your party, such as the cake, the dress, or the venue, or offer guidance, advice, and support to help make your dreams come true.

The Officiant

The officiant leads the religious ceremony or spiritual service of your quincañera. Choosing the right person to officiate your special day is an important decision, as they will guide you through meaningful rites and rituals.

This person will play a central role in your celebration, so choose someone who understands your beliefs, connects with you on a personal level, and can lead a ceremony that is both inspiring and memorable.

Here are some tips on selecting the officiant for your quinceañera:

Consider your personal beliefs
The first step in choosing an officiant is to consider your own beliefs and values. Whether you come from a religious, spiritual, or secular background, select someone who shares your views and can create a ceremony that reflects your personal beliefs

Look within your community
In many cases, the officiant is a priest, pastor, deacon, or religious leader from your community or place of worship. If you have a close relationship with someone in this role, consider asking them to officiate. Alternatively, you could also ask a family friend, mentor, or relative who is knowledgeable about your belief system.

Meet with potential officiants
Before making a decision, arrange a meeting with potential officiants to discuss your vision for the ceremony. This will help you get a sense of their personality, communication style, and approach to the ceremony. Make sure you feel comfortable and connected with the person who will be guiding you through this significant milestone

Confirm availability and fees
Make sure they're available on your chosen date and discuss any fees or expenses associated with their services. Keep in mind that some religious officiants may require you to complete a course or participate in special preparations leading up to your quinceañera.

Communicate your expectations
Share your ideas and expectations for the ceremony with your officiant, including any specific readings, prayers, or rituals you would like to include. In the case of Catholic quinceañeras, there may already be a standard format in place.

Ceremony participants

By inviting friends, family, and loved ones to participate in various roles and rituals, you can make your quinceañera even more personalized and heartfelt.

Consider the people who have had a significant impact on your life and have supported you throughout your journey. By involving them in your quinceañera, you can create a deep and meaningful connection that honors the love, guidance, and friendship they have provided. Here are some options for ceremony participants on your special day:

- **Readers**: Choose a few close friends or family members to read passages, poems, or quotes that hold special meaning to you. These readings can be religious, spiritual, or secular in nature, and should reflect your personal beliefs and the theme of your quinceañera.

- **Candle Lighters**: The candle lighting ceremony is a beautiful tradition that symbolizes the influence of loved ones in your life. Invite 15 special people (one for each year of your life) to light a candle and say a few words or share a memory about your relationship. You may even choose a group of people to light one candle, or dedicate a candle to someone in memoriam. This is a touching way to honor those who have shaped your journey and express your gratitude for their support.

- **Gift Presenters**: During the ceremony, it's customary for parents, madrinas, or padrinos to present the quinceañera with symbolic gifts, such as a tiara, cross, or Bible. Consider asking other loved ones to present additional gifts that hold personal significance, like a special piece of jewelry, a family heirloom, or a handwritten letter.

- **Musical Performers**: If you have friends or family members who are talented musicians, singers, or dancers, invite them to perform during your ceremony or reception.

- **Blessings and Prayers**: Invite your close friends and family members to offer their blessings or prayers for your future during the ceremony. This can be done individually or as a group and is a beautiful way to involve your loved ones in your special day.

Guests

Your guests are all the family members, friends, and loved ones who will share in the celebration with you. You'll want to consider factors like the size of your guest list, relationships, and any special accommodations needed to ensure that all your guests feel welcome and included. In the chapter, "Guest Lists & Communications" we'll provide tips for creating invitations, managing RSVPs, and more to make sure your guest etiquette is on point!

Vendors & Professional Help

While your friends and family play a vital role in your quince, it's also essential to have a team of experienced professionals to ensure that your celebration goes smoothly. From caterers and photographers to DJs and event planners, these experts will help bring your vision to life.

If you hire an event planner, they will likely coordinate with vendors and negotiate contracts as part of their fee. If you don't have an event planner but have chosen a venue, it's a great idea to ask the venue staff for recommendations for vendors. Many venues have established relationships with local vendors, including caterers, DJs, bands, and MCs. Their recommendations can help you find reliable and professional services that have already been tried and tested by other clients.

Professional recommendations can save you a lot of time and effort in your search for the right vendors. Additionally, using the venue's preferred vendors may lead to a smoother event, as they will already be familiar with the venue's layout and policies.

However, always remember to do your own research and compare the recommended vendors to others in the area. Reading reviews, checking portfolios, and conducting interviews can help you make an informed decision.

Here are some key professionals and vendors you may want to consider for your quinceañera. We will cover these topics in greater detail in later chapters of this book:

- **Caterer**: Great food is a must at any celebration! Choose a reputable caterer who can provide delicious cuisine that reflects your personal taste and style.

- **Choreographer**: A choreographer will typically create dance routines for the group waltz and the surprise dance.

- **DJ or Band**: Music sets the tone for your party, so find a DJ or band that can create the perfect atmosphere and keep your guests dancing all night long.

- **Event Planner**: Hiring an event planner can be a lifesaver, especially if you're feeling overwhelmed by the planning process. They'll handle the logistics, coordinate with vendors, and help you stay on track with your timeline and budget. They can also help coordinate all your activities on the day of your quince.

- **Florist**: Beautiful flowers can elevate your quinceañera décor to the next level. Work with a florist who understands your vision and can create arrangements that complement your theme and color palette.

- **Master of Ceremonies (MC or Emcee)**: A master of ceremonies, or MC, is responsible for hosting an event and keeping the program on schedule. They will make announcements, introduce performers, speeches, and toasts, guide guests through the various activities and traditions of the celebration, and otherwise keep the event flowing smoothly.

- **Photographer and/or Videographer**: Your quinceañera is a once-in-a-lifetime event, so make sure to capture the memories with a skilled photographer and/or videographer.

- **Hairstylist and Makeup Artist**: Look and feel your best on your special day by hiring a professional hair and makeup artist. Schedule a trial before the event to ensure you're happy with the final result.

- **Graphic Designer**: A skilled graphic designer can help create a cohesive look for the celebration, from designing invitations and printed materials to creating a website. Professional-looking printed materials add a touch of elegance and sophistication to the celebration.

- **Calligrapher**: A calligrapher can add a personal and memorable touch to the event's invitations, programs, and other printed materials.

- **Rentals**: Depending on your venue, you may need to rent items like tables, chairs, linens, and tableware. Find a reliable rental company that offers a wide selection and can accommodate your specific needs.

CHAPTER THREE

From Ceremony to Reception

THERE ARE USUALLY TWO main parts to a quinceañera: the ceremony and the reception. These can vary in style and format and different activities can occur in each program. You can decide which traditions you want to observe or create new ones of your own.

The ceremony is traditionally a religious service. It is often a Catholic Mass, but could also be another denomination, non-denominational, interfaith, or secular. Some quinceañeras opt not to have a ceremony. The ceremony is typically followed by the reception, also known as a *fiesta*, which is a lively party that is considered by many to be the main event.

The Ceremony (*La Ceremonia*)

The quinceañera ceremony traditionally takes place in a Catholic church or house of worship. However, the ceremony may also take place at the site of the reception, or another of your choosing, and can be adapted to suit your family's beliefs and traditions. Some families forgo a religious ceremony altogether.

The following is an example of a quinceañera ceremony:

The Procession

The ceremony begins with a procession, where the quinceañera, her court of honor, and family members walk down the aisle to take their seats.

The Ceremony

The officiant will lead the group in prayers and readings from the Bible. A Catholic Mass begins with the Liturgy of the Word, during which the quinceañera may serve as the lector for at least one of the readings if she has prepared them.

The quinceañera may offer a special prayer or reflection, thanking God for the blessings in her life and asking for guidance in her journey to adulthood.

After the Liturgy of the Word, the quinceañera commits to God and the Blessed Virgin to live out the rest of her life according to the teachings of Christ and the Church by renewing her baptismal promises.

The quinceañera is then presented with signs of faith such as a medal, Bible, rosary, or prayer book, which have been blessed and may be given to her.

The Presentation

The father or another family member may accompany the quinceañera to the altar and present her to the community, symbolizing her entrance into womanhood. The quinceañera may also offer a bouquet to the Virgin Mary or another saint, as a symbol of gratitude and devotion.

The Homily or Sermon

After the presentation, the priest or officiant may offer a homily or sermon, encouraging the quinceañera to embrace her responsibilities as a young adult and to seek guidance and support from her family and community.

The Blessing
The ceremony concludes with a blessing and the signing of the quinceañera's certificate of completion of religious education. The quinceañera and her court of honor then exit the church, to continue the celebration at the reception.

The Reception (*La Recepción*)

After the ceremony, guests gather for the main event — the reception! This is where everyone can enjoy food, music, and dancing. It's the true heart of the quinceañera, a time to celebrate with family and friends, have fun, and make treasured memories.

While some of the following activities and traditions are typically observed, each quince is unique. Feel free to mix and match the parts that resonate with you, and create a celebration that's truly yours.

The Presentation (*La Presentación*) or Grand Entrance
The quinceañera is formally introduced to guests, usually by the MC or a family member. It's an opportunity to see everyone's beautiful attire and take photos. The order of the grand entrance can vary, but it generally follows this sequence:

- The parents of the celebrant are introduced first, often to a special song that holds significance for the family.

- The court, consisting of the damas and chambelanes, is then introduced, usually in pairs or groups.

- The quinceañera is typically the last to be introduced. She makes her grand entrance, often to a song of her choice.

The Crowning (*La Coronación*)

The coronation can take place during the religious service, before the reception, or at the reception. During the coronation, the quinceañera is presented with a tiara, which is placed on her head by her parents or godparents. A special song or piece of music may be played during the ceremony.

The quinceañera may also be presented with a scepter, which represents her new authority as a young woman, as well as a Bible or prayer book, which represents her faith and her commitment to living a good and virtuous life. The ceremony may include a special prayer or blessing offered by the officiant.

The Last Doll (*La Última Muñeca*)

The quinceañera is presented with a doll, representing her last toy as she leaves childhood behind. Sometimes instead of a doll, a stuffed bear may be given. She may choose to pass the doll on to a younger sibling or retain it as a keepsake.

The Changing of the Shoes (*El Cambio de Zapatos*)

The quinceañera's father or a significant figure replaces her flat shoes with high heels, symbolizing her transition into womanhood.

The Father-Daughter Dance (*El Baile con Papá*)

The quinceañera shares a special dance with her father or another important male figure, highlighting their bond and the support she receives from her family.

The Mother-Daughter Dance (*El Baile con Mamá*)

A mother-daughter dance is a beautiful way to celebrate the bond between the quinceañera and her mother or another important female figure.

The Goddaughter-Godfather Dance
(*El Baile con el Padrino*)

The quinceañera shares a special moment with her godfather(s), highlighting the important role he plays in her life and the guidance he has provided.

The Goddaughter-Godmother Dance
(*El Baile con la Madrina*)

This special moment can be a touching tribute to the love and care that her godmother(s) has shown the quinceañera.

The Group Waltz (*El Vals*)

The quinceañera and her Court of Honor perform a choreographed waltz. This is often a highlight of the celebration, showcasing the celebrant and her closest friends and family members.

The Toast (*El Brindis*)

Family members and close friends make toasts to the quinceañera to celebrate her and share well-wishes for her future. The toasts are heartfelt and filled with anecdotes and memories of the quinceañera's childhood.

Thank You Speech

The quinceañera gives a speech thanking her loved ones for their support and reflecting on the significance of this milestone in her life. The speech is an opportunity for the quinceañera to share her thoughts, dreams, and aspirations for the future, as well as a chance to show her appreciation to those who have supported her throughout her life.

15 Candles Ceremony

The quinceañera dedicates 15 candles to 15 important people in her life. The candles can represent family members, friends, or mentors who have played significant roles in her life. This is a way to show gratitude and respect to those who have supported the quinceañera throughout her life.

Each candle is lit during the ceremony, and the quinceañera gives a speech or reads a letter to honor the person the candle represents. If the person or people are present, they may be invited up to light the candle with the quinceañera. This ceremony can also take the place of a thank you speech.

The Surprise Dance (*El Baile Sorpresa*)
This dance is kept a secret until the big day, as a fun and unexpected treat for the guests. The surprise dance can be any style or genre you like, and offers an opportunity for you, the quinceañera, to showcase your unique personality and have a blast with your court of honor.

The Cutting of the Cake (*El Corte del Pastel*)
The quinceañera cuts her cake and shares it with her guests, symbolizing the sweetness of the celebration.

The Dinner
The quinceañera dinner can occur before or after the quinceañera's presentation. The dinner may be formal or informal. It typically includes a variety of dishes, from appetizers to main courses and desserts, and it's a chance for the family to showcase their culinary traditions and hospitality.

Gifts
The celebrant will usually receive a variety of gifts from her family and friends, such as jewelry, religious items, money, or other sentimental items. Religious gifts may also be presented during the preceding religious ceremony if there is one. During the reception, the presentation of gifts is often accompanied by speeches or other tributes, and it is a meaningful part of the celebration that symbolizes the love and support of those closest to the quinceañera.

- **Tiara**: The tiara usually replaces a headpiece worn by the quinceañera until she is crowned.

- **Scepter**: The scepter is placed in the hand of the quinceañera to symbolize her taking on adult roles as well as the authority that goes with her new position in the family and society.

- **Prayer Book or Bible**: A prayer book or Bible is given to the quinceañera as a resource to keep the word of God in her life.

- **Ring or Bracelet**: A ring or bracelet is given to symbolize the never-ending circle of life, the never-ending cycle of womanhood, and her future contributions.

- **Rosary**: Rosary beads are often given in combination with the Bible as a useful tool in the prayer life of a young Catholic woman.

- **Bouquet**: A bouquet may be used if a mass service is held to place at the Altar of the Virgin Maria as a gift of gratitude.

- **Headpiece**: A headpiece is worn as an adornment until replaced by the tiara.

- **Quinceañera Doll**: The "last doll" is given away to a younger female family member as a symbol of leaving her childhood behind, but may also be kept as a souvenir.

- **Pillows**: Several pillows are often used during a quinceañera ceremony, including one for kneeling during the service, one for carrying her new shoes, and one for the tiara she receives.

* **Recuerdos**: Small party favors that are given to the guests as thanks for their attendance. The word *recuerdo* means "memory" or "souvenir" in Spanish, and are intended to be a keepsake that guests can take home with them to remember the special occasion. Some examples or *recuerdos* include candles, a small box of sweets, or picture frames.

    The Party (*La Fiesta*) The dance floor opens up to everyone, and the celebration continues with music, dancing, and laughter.

The Order of Events: A Sample Timeline

The following is an example of the order of events that may occur on the day of a quinceañera:

DAY-OF PREP
6 AM — 10 AM
• Breakfast
• Hair and Makeup

10 AM — 12 PM
• The Court of Honor (*Corte de Honor*) arrives
• Photographer and/or videographer arrive
• Capture the quinceañera getting ready

12 PM — 3 PM
• Party bus/limo arrives
• Drive to photoshoot locations
• Lunch/Snacks

3 PM — 4 PM
• Arrive at the ceremony location
• Apply touchups

THE CEREMONY (*LA CEREMONIA*)
4 PM — 5 PM
• Church ceremony
• Leave for the reception
• (Some celebrants may opt to have a photo shoot at additional, pre-determined locations between The Ceremony and The Reception)

THE RECEPTION (*LA RECEPCIÓN*)
5 PM — 7:30 PM
• Dinner

7:30 PM — 9 PM
• Grand Entrance (*Baile de entrada*)
• The Crowning (*La Coronación*)
• The Last Doll (*La Ultima Muñeca*)
• The Changing of the Shoes (*Cambio de Zapatillas*)
• The Father–Daughter Dance (*El Baile con Papá*)
• The Mother–Daughter Dance (*El Baile con Mamá*)
• The Group Waltz (*El Baile el Vals*)
• Thank You Speech and Toasts (*El Brindis*)
• Surprise Dance (*Baile Sopresa*)

9 PM
• Change back into your quinceañera dress
• Cake cutting
• Take pictures with guests

9:30 PM — 12 AM
• Everybody dance!

CHAPTER FOUR

Develop Your Vision

Y OUR VISION SETS THE foundation for the planning process and helps you stay organized, inspired, and focused. It establishes the direction for your quinceañera and enables you to make decisions with confidence.

Documenting your vision with an inspiration board can make it easier to communicate your ideas and expectations to your family, friends, and vendors. It ensures everyone is on the same page, serves as a reminder of your ultimate goal, and keeps you aligned on the overall vision.

Pick a theme

Your theme should reflect your personality in some way. It can be as simple or as elaborate as you want, and can be inspired by your favorite color, hobby, or cultural tradition. A theme can tie together all aspects of the celebration, from the invitations and decorations to the dress and entertainment. Here are some prompts to help you choose a theme that truly reflects your personality and interests:

Reflect on your interests

Begin by thinking about what you love most. Are you a bookworm, a movie buff, or a fashionista? Do you have a favorite hobby, sport, or travel destination? Make a list of your interests to help you brainstorm potential theme ideas.

If you're into anime, punk rock, and boxing, you can tie that into your theme. Maybe your quinceañera will feature you with pink hair, wearing boxing shoes, and doing your surprise dance to "Let's Dance" by The Ramones!

Consider your personal style

Are you drawn to vintage charm or modern elegance? Do you prefer bold and colorful or soft and romantic? Use your personal style as a starting point to help you narrow down your theme choices.

Look for inspiration

Start by browsing magazines, social media, and websites for quinceañera ideas that catch your eye. Save images and create a mood board, either physically or digitally, to gather all your favorite looks in one place. This will help you see what styles and themes you're naturally drawn to.

Think about the location and season

The venue and time of year can influence your theme selection. For example, an outdoor garden party might be perfect for a spring or summer celebration, while a winter wonderland theme could be a great fit for a colder month.

Consult with friends and family

Share your ideas with those closest to you and ask for their input. They might have creative suggestions or insights into what would best represent you and your personality.

Be true to yourself
Ultimately, the most important factor in choosing a theme is that it feels true to who you are. Choose a theme that makes you feel excited, happy, and confident.

Brainstorm theme ideas

Once you've selected your theme, the fun really begins! Your theme will help you make decisions on everything from the invitations and decorations to the dress and the entertainment.

Here are some fun and fabulous theme ideas. You can also mix and match elements from different themes. Let your imagination take the lead!

- **Hollywood Glamour**: Roll out the red carpet and create a glitzy, Oscars-inspired party with gold accents, a photo backdrop, and movie-themed table settings.

- **Fairytale Ball**: Transport your guests to a storybook world featuring enchanting blue and silver hues, sparkling decorations, and regal touches. Revel in the magic of a grand ballroom adorned with crystal chandeliers and whimsical accents like a horse-drawn carriage.

- **Masquerade Ball**: Immerse your guests in a mysterious, elegant world with masks, lavish decorations, and a royal color palette like deep purples, reds, or blues.

- **Garden Party**: Create a magical atmosphere with lush greenery, blossoming flowers, and hidden pathways. Add vintage keys, antique books, and Victorian-style accents to the charming setting.

- **By the Shore**: Decorate with delicate seashells, soft sandy tones, and hints of ocean blues and greens. Incorporate beach-inspired elements, such as driftwood, sea glass, and nautical accents, to create a coastal paradise.

- **Parisian Chic**: Channel the elegance and romance of Paris with Eiffel Tower decorations, a black-and-white color scheme, and classic French pastries.

- **Winter Wonderland**: Step into a frosty, sparkling wonderland with snowy decorations, icy blue hues, faux fur accents, and crystal centerpieces.

- **Tropical Escape**: Turn your quince into a vibrant beach getaway with palm trees, exotic flowers, and bright colors, along with a tiki bar and fruit cocktails.

- **Fiesta**: Celebrate with a lively and colorful Mexican-inspired party, complete with *papel picado* decorations, delicious traditional foods, and a mariachi band.

- **Tea Party**: Host a charming afternoon tea with delicate china, pastel colors, beautiful floral arrangements, and finger sandwiches.

- **Carnival**: Bring the excitement of a carnival to your quince with fun games, bright colors, festive treats, and a carousel-inspired cake

- **Alice in Wonderland**: Fall down the rabbit hole into a whimsical and quirky world filled with harlequin patterns, oversized props, and an elaborate Mad Hatter's tea party.

- **Starry Night**: Create a celestial celebration with galaxy-inspired decor, twinkling lights, and shades of purple and blue, along with star-shaped treats.

- **Sunflower Splendor**: Incorporate vibrant sunflower arrangements, rustic décor, and warm yellow accents for a cheerful and inviting atmosphere.

- **Great Gatsby**: Step back in time to the glamorous 1920s with art deco gold and black decor and vintage accessories, like feathered headbands and beaded dresses.

- **The 1950s**: Stage a fun 1950s-inspired sock hop, complete with retro diner decor, jukebox, records, and a Thunderbird photo prop.

Select a color palette

Creating the perfect color palette for your quinceañera is all about finding the right combination of colors that express your personality and complement your chosen theme. Here are some steps to guide you through the process:

Look for inspiration
Browse through magazines, websites, and social media to gather ideas and inspiration for your color palette.

Start with a color scheme
Choose two to three main colors that reflect your theme and personal style. Think about the mood you want to create at your celebration. Lighter colors often evoke a romantic and delicate feeling, while bolder colors can make a statement and add energy to your event.

To add depth and visual interest to your palette, incorporate one or two accent colors that contrast or complement your main colors. These can be used in smaller decorative elements, such as table settings, centerpieces, or party favors.

Consider the season
The time of year can influence your color choices. Spring and summer celebrations may call for pastels or bright hues, while a fall event might inspire deeper, richer colors like burgundy, amber, and gold, and winter might call for cooler colors like blue, white, and silver.

Consider the location
You can use your surroundings to pick up color cues. For a beach or tropical location, you might consider coral, turquoise, and sunshine yellow. For a desert location, you might draw inspiration from a photo at sunset with earthen tones like sage green, ochre, peach, and mauve.

Consider the culture
If your quinceañera is inspired by your heritage, think about incorporating those traditional colors or patterns into your color palette. For example, a Mexican, charro-themed celebration might incorporate red, green, and white.

Mix and match
Don't be afraid to mix and match. You can create a unique and eye-catching color palette by combining unexpected colors or patterns. Just be sure to keep the overall vibe in mind when making your choices.

Be mindful of balance and harmony
As you choose your colors, strive for a balanced and harmonious look. Too many colors can make your quinceañera feel visually overwhelming. Aim for a cohesive color palette that highlights your theme without going overboard.

Palette inspiration

Check out these beautiful color palette ideas and the vibes they create. These are just a few color palette ideas to get your creative juices flowing:

- **Blush, gold, and ivory**: This dreamy and romantic combo oozes sophistication and charm. Ideal for a fairytale or vintage-inspired quinceañera, it represents love and timeless elegance.

- **Turquoise, coral, and white**: Bright and lively, this color palette captures the essence of a tropical or beach-themed celebration. It's all about fun and happiness, perfect for the carefree and adventurous girl.

- **Lavender, sage green, and silver**: Serene and calming, this lovely color mix is perfect for a garden or enchanted forest-themed quinceañera. It speaks of tranquility and harmony, symbolizing your connection to nature and inner peace.

- **Navy blue, burgundy, and gold**: Rich and luxurious, this color palette projects glamour and is perfect for a Hollywood-inspired event. It conveys a sense of opulence and sophistication, reflecting confidence and ambition.

- **Rose gold, dusty rose, and gray**: This chic color combo is great for a modern or minimalist quinceañera. It evokes warmth and refined elegance, striking the right balance between tradition and contemporary style.

- **Emerald green, black, and gold**: Bold and mysterious, this striking color palette is perfect for a masquerade or

Gatsby-themed party. It radiates intrigue and daring, perfect for a girl with a sense of adventure.

Set the Scene

The lighting and decor sets the mood for your quince. You can create a cohesive and enchanting atmosphere through the selection of materials, textures, lighting, table settings, floral arrangements, and backdrops. Think about how all the elements come together to create a sense of your theme.

Table settings
Select tableware, glassware, and flatware that coordinate with your color palette and theme. You can also add personalized touches like custom napkins, menu cards, or place cards.

Centerpieces and floral arrangements
Choose flowers and centerpieces that coordinate with your color palette and reflect your theme. You can be creative with your floral arrangements by using unique vases, incorporating non-floral elements, or creating a mix of different centerpiece styles. You don't need to limit yourself to fresh flowers either. Paper, artificial flowers and plants, and props can all be used to dramatic effect.

Backdrops and photo areas
Create an instagrammable backdrop or photo area that captures the spirit of your theme. This can be a simple wall decorated with balloons and streamers or an elaborate scene that transports your guests to another setting.

Lighting
The right lighting can set the mood and highlight your theme. Use candles, fairy lights, or lanterns to create a warm and inviting

atmosphere. For a more dramatic effect, consider using colored lighting or a light projection that complements your theme.

Décor Themes Ideas

Here are some examples of how decor can be used to support various themes:

- **Enchanted Forest:** Use lush greenery, twinkling fairy lights, and rustic wooden elements to create a magical woodland setting. Drape tables in earth tones, and use moss-covered centerpieces and lanterns to evoke a sense of mystery and enchantment.

- **Vintage Glamour:** Incorporate materials like lace, satin, and pearls in your decor. Use soft, romantic lighting, such as chandeliers or candles, to create an intimate atmosphere. Include vintage china and crystal glassware, and floral arrangements featuring classic blooms like roses or peonies.

- **Under the Sea:** Play with different shades of blue and green for table linens and chair covers. Use materials like shimmering organza or tulle to create a sense of flowing water. Incorporate seashells, starfish, and faux coral into your centerpieces and table settings.

- **Rustic Chic:** Focus on natural materials like wood, burlap, and twine. Use wooden pallets or barrels for displays, and incorporate wildflowers into your floral arrangements. Dress tables with burlap runners and simple white linens. Use mason jars or galvanized metal buckets as vases or candle holders.

- **Hollywood Glam:** Combine rich textures like velvet or

satin with metallic accents in gold or silver. Use dramatic lighting, such as spotlights or uplights, to create a sense of drama and excitement. Set tables with elegant chargers, sparkling glassware, and feathered centerpieces. Create a dramatic red carpet entrance.

Create an Inspiration Board

An inspiration board is a collection of images, colors, materials, and anything else that sparks your creativity and reflects the vision you have for your special day.

Creating an inspiration board is a fun and effective way to keep your ideas organized and share them with other people. Here are tips on how to create an inspiration board:

Choose a method
Start by gathering materials for your inspiration board. You can use a physical cork or foam board, or a digital board like Pinterest, Canva, Mural, or Miro. You can use a notebook or a folder. Choose whatever method works best for you and your planning style.

Collect inspiration
Begin collecting images, colors, patterns, and anything else that resonates with your quinceañera theme and style. Look for inspiration in magazines, online, or by visiting local stores and events. Don't limit yourself — the more inspiration you gather, the better!

Organize your ideas
Once you've collected plenty of inspiration, it's time to organize it. Group similar ideas together, such as color palettes, themes, or specific elements like decor or outfits. This will help you identify patterns and preferences that can guide your planning decisions.

Refine your vision

As you organize your inspiration board, you may notice some ideas that stand out more than others or that certain elements don't quite fit with the overall vibe. Refine your vision by removing anything that doesn't align with your desired theme or style.

Share your board

Share your inspiration board with your team, vendors, and anyone else involved in your quinceañera planning. This will help them understand your vision and ensure everyone is on the same page as they work to bring your ideas to life.

Update and revise

Your inspiration board is not set in stone. As you progress through the planning process, you may discover new ideas and inspiration. Update and revise your board as needed to keep it current and reflective of your evolving vision.

CHAPTER FIVE

Budget Like a Pro

IT'S ESSENTIAL TO HAVE a clear understanding of your budget. Setting up a realistic budget doesn't mean sacrificing the magic of your quinceañera. A well-planned budget will free you to focus on making your vision a reality with the resources that are available to you. It's about making informed decisions, prioritizing what truly matters, and finding creative ways to bring your vision to life in a feasible way.

You don't need anything fancier than a lined notebook or a spreadsheet to plan and track a budget. You can use a free online spreadsheet like Google Sheets, which has all the functionality you need. Another option is a notebook planner like Oh Happy Day Press' *Essential Quinceañera Planner* which has detailed worksheets that can help you plan, track, and manage a budget with categories specific to quinceañeras.

Determine your total budget

Start by discussing how much money is available for your quince. Consider any contributions from family members, madrinas, and padrinos, as well as any savings you may have. Be sure to have an honest conversation about what is financially feasible for your family.

List your expenses
Create a comprehensive list of all the potential expenses for your quince, including venue, attire, catering, entertainment, decorations, invitations, and transportation. Don't forget about smaller items like favors, thank-you cards, and gratuities for vendors.

Research costs
Do some research to get a general idea of the costs associated with each item on your list. This may involve browsing websites, contacting vendors, or asking friends and family members for recommendations.

Prioritize
With a clear understanding of the costs, it's time to prioritize your expenses. Determine which aspects of your quince are most important to you, and allocate a larger portion of your budget to those items. Be prepared to make compromises or find creative solutions for less essential elements.

Allocate funds
Based on your priorities and research, allocate a specific amount of money to each item on your list. Make sure the total matches your predetermined budget. This will serve as your spending guideline throughout the planning process.

Keep Track of Your Expenses

As you make purchases and book vendors, keep track of your spending. This will help you stay within your budget and make necessary adjustments if you start to overspend in a particular area.

Here are some tips to help you effectively monitor and manage your quinceañera expenses:

Save receipts and invoices

Keep all receipts and invoices from your purchases and vendor bookings in a safe place, such as a dedicated folder or binder. This will make it easy to refer back to them when you're updating your spreadsheet and ensure you have accurate records. A spreadsheet is a powerful tool that can help you stay on top of expenses. We will cover this more in the next section.

Categorize your expenses

Organize your expenses into categories, such as attire, food, entertainment, and decorations. This will help you identify areas where you may be overspending and make it easier to reallocate funds if needed.

Set reminders for payment deadlines

Missing a payment deadline can result in late fees or even the cancellation of a vendor booking. Use a calendar or reminder app to schedule alerts for upcoming payment due dates.

Review your budget periodically

Regularly review your budget to assess your progress and make any necessary adjustments. This will help you stay on track and ensure you're making the most of your available funds.

Be prepared for unexpected expenses

It's always a good idea to set aside a small contingency fund for unforeseen costs that may arise during the planning process. This will give you some wiggle room in your budget and help you avoid stress if unexpected expenses come up.

Make a spreadsheet

One of the most useful tools to help you set up a budget and track your expenses is to use software called a spreadsheet.

You can use spreadsheet software like Microsoft Excel, Google Sheets, Apple Numbers, or a budgeting app like Mint (free) or You Need a Budget (YNAB) (paid). This will help you monitor your spending and make adjustments if necessary.

A spreadsheet helps you organize information in meaningful ways. It presents information in rows and columns on a table. You enter information in different boxes, and the program will automatically keep everything neat.

For example, you might have a list of expenses, like the cost of the dress, venue rental, DJ, and decorations. You can use a spreadsheet to list each category with corresponding expenses.

This way, you can easily see how much you're spending on each category and track your total expenses. You can create formulas to do calculations, like adding up all the expenses to get subtotals by category, or the total cost across all categories.

However, a spreadsheet is only as good as the information you enter into it. Inaccurate data will give you an inaccurate picture of your spending. Make a habit of updating your budget spreadsheet every time you make a purchase or payment. This will help you stay on top of your expenses and prevent any surprises later on.

A spreadsheet can do more than just help you keep track of your budget and expenses. You can also use it to track information like contacts, vendors, guest lists, gifts, or your playlist. It's a really useful tool for staying organized and keeping all your information in one place!

There are many ways to set up spreadsheets. You can find many free templates online that will show you different approaches. Knowing how to create and manage spreadsheets is a great skill that you can use in other areas of your life, like at school or a job!

Here are examples of a budget and an expense tracker from Oh Happy Day Press' *The Essential Quinceañera Planner*. You can use them as references to set up your own budgeting system.

SAMPLE BUDGET: $10,000		
Category	**% Percent of Budget**	**Budget Amount**
Venue & Catering	40%	$4,000
Photography	15%	$1,500
Music	10%	$1,000
Flowers	10%	$1,000
Decor	10%	$1,000
Attire	5%	$500
Transportation	3%	$300
Stationery	3%	$300
Favors	2%	$200
Cake	2%	$200
Total Budget	100%	$10,000

Itemized budget

CATERING				
Item	Estimated	Actual	Difference	Notes
Reception Catering	$	$	$	
Waitstaff/Servers	$	$	$	
Beverages	$	$	$	
Cake	$	$	$	
Table/chair/linen rentals	$	$	$	
	$	$	$	
	$	$	$	
	$	$	$	
	$	$	$	
	$	$	$	
	$	$	$	
	$	$	$	
	$	$	$	
	$	$	$	
Total Reception	$	$	$	

PHOTOGRAPHY & VIDEOGRAPHY				
Item	Estimated	Actual	Difference	Notes
Photographer	$	$	$	
Videographer	$	$	$	
Photo albums	$	$	$	
	$	$	$	
	$	$	$	
	$	$	$	
	$	$	$	
	$	$	$	
Total Photo & Video	$	$	$	

Expense tracker

Smart Saving Tips and Negotiation Tricks

With a bit of bargain savvy, you can make the most of your quinceañera budget and still have an unforgettable event. Remember, it's not about how much you spend, but about making smart choices and finding creative ways to stretch your budget without sacrificing the important stuff.

Here are some ways you can make the most of your budget:

Prioritize your spending
Identify the most important aspects of your quinceañera and allocate a larger portion of your budget to those areas. This will help you focus your resources on what matters most to you while cutting back on less important expenses. If your dress is more important to you than the floral arrangements, knowing that will make it easier to make decisions when and if you need to cut costs. At the same time, let's say you find your dream dress on sale and have money left over from that category, then your priorities will tell you what to put the excess towards.

Comparison shop
Compare prices from multiple vendors and suppliers to find the best deals. Don't be afraid to negotiate with vendors for better prices or additional services. Many vendors are willing to work with your budget and may offer discounts or package deals.

Ask your friends and family if there's anyone in their network who can help. A personal relationship, even a tangential one, can lead to good deals. "My cousin knows a guy who DJs" or, "My aunt's co-worker's family owns a bakery," might lead you to a great resource. At the same time, just because a person is a friend of a friend doesn't mean you shouldn't vet them and ask them the same questions as you would any other vendor.

Practice the art of negotiation

When discussing prices with vendors, be polite but assertive. Let vendors and sellers know your budget constraints and ask if they can offer any discounts, package deals, or additional services at no extra cost. Remember, it never hurts to ask, and you might be surprised by the deals you can secure.

Do-It-Yourself (DIY)

Consider identifying some tasks you may be able to DIY, such as creating your own invitations or decorations.

You can also consider enlisting the help of talented family and friends who can contribute their skills to your celebration. Perhaps you have a tío who plays guitar and could provide musical entertainment for part of the evening, or a friend with nice handwriting who can help you address envelopes. You might ask a tía who makes killer empanadas to bring them as appetizers, or a cousin who's super organized to be your day-of event coordinator. It's a great way to get people involved and feel like they're contributing to making your day extra special with their unique strengths and talents.

Be flexible with dates and times

Choosing an off-peak season or a weekday for your quinceañera can result in significant savings on venue rental and other services. Vendors are often more willing to negotiate lower prices during less busy times.

Consider new businesses and talent

New businesses and people who are just starting out their careers may charge discounted rates for a chance to show what they can do. A good place to look for new talent is training schools. Cosmetology, hair salons, and culinary schools will often offer discounted services from students and trainees under the supervision of a teaching professional.

Borrow or rent items
Instead of buying everything new, consider borrowing items from friends or family or renting them from a party supply company. This can save you money on things like decorations, tableware, and attire.

Utilize social media
Follow your favorite vendors on social media to stay updated on special offers, promotions, or discounts. You might also discover new vendors or ideas through social media platforms like Instagram and Pinterest.

Keep an eye out for sales
Shop sales or clearance events to save money. There may be certain times of year, during and after holidays, when you can find great promotions and discounts.

Buy secondhand
Who doesn't love a good secondhand find? You can find great deals and unique items browsing thrift stores, garage sales, and online marketplaces. Shop secondhand, but do so strategically and with a curatorial eye. Secondhand is also great for DIY. With a bit of creativity, you can bring new life to pre-loved things.

CHAPTER SIX

Manage Like a Boss

Y OU'VE CREATED YOUR VISION, assembled your dream team, and learned to budget like a pro. Now, it's time to bring all the elements together so that everything runs smoothly and according to plan. In this chapter, we'll guide you through the project management skills you'll need to make your quinceañera a smooth operation. We'll talk timelines, and task delegation, and introduce you to helpful tools that'll keep your plans and tasks on track.

Developing these skills will enable you to work with a team to make your quinceañera a success. So, let's roll up our sleeves and learn to manage your quince like a boss!

Create a timeline

A well-structured timeline will give you a clear roadmap to follow as you plan your quinceañera. It helps you keep track of every task and milestone, ensuring nothing slips through the cracks. It'll reduce stress, and ensure your celebration comes together seamlessly. So, grab your calendar, and let's start building your timeline!

Start with the big picture
Begin by listing all the major milestones leading up to your quinceañera, such as selecting a venue, choosing a dress, and sending out invitations. Assign a target completion date for each milestone, working backward from your quinceañera date.

Break it down into smaller tasks
Once you've outlined the major milestones, break them down into smaller tasks. For example, choosing a dress may involve researching styles, scheduling dress appointments, and attending fittings. Assign deadlines for each task to keep yourself on track.

Be flexible
Remember, your timeline is a living document. As you progress with your planning, you may need to adjust some deadlines or tasks. Stay flexible and be prepared to make changes as needed.

Share your timeline
Make sure your family, friends, and vendors are aware of your timeline and their responsibilities. This will help ensure everyone is on the same page and working together towards a common goal.

Use helpful tools
There are plenty of tools and apps available to help you create and manage your timelines, such as Google Sheets, Trello, or Asana. Choose a tool that suits your style and needs, and don't be afraid to explore different options to find the perfect fit.

Regularly review and update your timeline
Make a habit of reviewing your timeline regularly to stay on top of your progress and make any necessary adjustments. Celebrate your achievements along the way and remember that you're one step closer to your dream quinceañera!

Sample timeline

Ideally, you'll begin planning a full year before the date of your quince. Many venues and professionals get booked in advance, particularly during popular seasons like spring, and around holidays. If you want to ensure that you get your first choice and the best price, remember to reserve early. The following is a sample timeline for reference to help you plan:

12+ Months Before:
- Set a date
- Set a budget
- Hire a planner
- Make a guest list
- Choose a Court of Honor
- Gather inspiration
- Decide on a theme
- Book ceremony and reception venue
- Choose an officiant
- Book caterer
- Research key vendors

11 Months Before:
- Select color palette
- Hire a photographer and videographer
- Hire a band / DJ / entertainment for the reception

10 Months Before:
- Start shopping for a gown
- Secure accommodations for yourself and your guests

9 Months Before:
- Buy quinceañera gown

- Send save-the-date cards
- Book florist
- Book choreographer

8 Months Before:
- Choose Damas' dresses
- Schedule fittings within the month

7 Months Before:
- Hire ceremony musicians
- Hire reception musicians
- Order rental items, props, decor

6 Months Before:
- Book transport for guests
- Book transport for you and the Court
- Book lighting technician
- Book cake tasting
- Hire invitation designer

5 Months Before:
- Devise reception timeline

4 Months Before:
- Final tasting with the caterer
- Choose cake
- Select chambelanes' attire and schedule fittings
- Hair and makeup trial

3 Months Before:
- First gown fitting
- Order invitations
- Hire calligrapher
- Finalize menu

- Choose Court favors
- Write thank you speech
- Meet with Officiant

2 Months Before:
- Second dress fitting
- Send invitations
- Buy Court favors
- Do floral mock-ups with the florist
- Give the song list to the band or DJ

1 Month Before:
- Assemble gift bags
- Pay vendors in full
- Create a seating chart
- Final venue walkthrough
- Practice speech out loud
- Put cash tips into envelopes

1-2 Weeks Before:
- Final gown fitting
- Refresh hair color
- Get eyebrows done
- Manicure/pedicure
- Follow up with late RSVPs
- Practice speech out loud

The Night Before:
- Eat a healthy meal
- Get a good night's sleep
- Pack everything to go

The Day Of:
- Eat breakfast

- Drink water
- Take your gown out of the bag
- Lay out all items for the photographer to capture
- Enjoy your quinceañera!

Within One Month After Your Quinceañera:
- Log gifts
- Get thank you cards and postage stamps
- Write thank you notes and send them — the sooner this is done, the better
- Pat yourself on the back for a job well done!

You don't need any special tools to create a timeline. A notebook is more than enough. If you're comfortable working with spreadsheets, they can be fantastic for making timelines as well. Oh Happy Day Press' *The Essential Quinceañera Planner* also has a detailed sample timeline and checklist along with blank worksheets you can use to customize the details of your own quinceañera. Whatever you decide, find a tool that you like working with, because you are going to be spending a lot of time with it!

Make "SMART" goals

SMART goals are a great technique that can help you achieve your goals. SMART stands for Specific, Measurable, Achievable, Relevant, and Time-bound.

When you set a SMART goal, you are defining exactly what you want to accomplish, how you will measure your progress, and when you want to achieve it. This clarity helps you stay focused and motivated and makes it easier to track your progress along the way.

To make a goal SMART, start by being *specific* about what you want to achieve. Instead of saying, "I want to buy a dress," you can say, "I want to buy a blue ballgown with a sequined bodice for less than $200 by May 31st." This gives you a clear target to aim for, and a timeline to work within.

Next, make sure your goal is *measurable*. This means breaking it down into smaller steps that you can track along the way. For example, if your goal is to save $1,000 in 6 months, you could break it down into a weekly savings plan of $40 per week and track your progress each week.

Your goal should be *achievable*. While it's great to aim high, you don't want to set yourself up for failure by setting an unrealistic goal. Make sure your goal is challenging but still within reach.

Your goal should be *relevant* to your quinceañera. This is where you ask if this is something you truly need to do that aligns with your overall priorities and vision. For example, let's say you want to set up a website for your quinceañera and find that it is a little beyond your abilities. That might motivate you to take a class to learn how to code in HTML, but while it's a very worthwhile goal, it's not relevant to your quinceañera.

Finally, make your goal *time-bound* by setting a specific deadline for when you want to achieve it. This helps create a sense of urgency and gives you a clear timeline to work within.

By setting SMART goals, you can turn your dreams into achievable targets and take concrete steps toward making them a reality.

Delegate tasks and set due dates

It's important to share responsibilities and set due dates to keep everyone on track. This way, your team can help you out, and everyone can be involved in making your big day a success.

Once you know what your goals are, break them down into the steps you need to take to achieve those goals. These are your tasks. Planning a quinceañera is a team effort and you will not be able to do everything yourself. You will need to delegate.

Decide which tasks can be shared with your team members. Think about what they're good at, what they like to do, and when they're available. Make sure they're on board with the plan and that everyone knows what they need to do, and what's expected of them.

Be clear when sharing tasks

When you give a task to someone, be clear about what needs to be done, what you want to achieve, and when it should be finished. Make it easy for your team members to ask questions or get help if they need it.

You can say something like, "Emma, I really appreciate you helping out with the decorations. Can I make you in charge of making the list of items we need by Friday so I can place my orders next week? And please let me know if you have any questions or if there's anything I can do to help you."

Set due dates

This is where your timeline and calendar come in. Due dates help everyone stay focused and responsible. Be sure to give people enough time to finish their tasks without feeling stressed.

When you set a due date, think about how long the task will take and when your team members are available. Once you set a due date for the goal you can work backwards to figure out the due date for each task.

Factor in dependencies

A dependency is a task that must be completed before the next one can begin. If you're not mindful of dependencies, sometimes they can stop you from progressing to the next task and meeting your overall target.

Here are examples of dependencies related to preparing for the surprise dance:

Tasks:

1. Choose a song for the surprise dance

2. Choreograph the dance
3. Practice the dance with the court
4. Decide on costumes for the surprise dance

Dependencies:
1. Task 1 must be completed before Task 2 can begin
2. Task 2 must be completed before Task 3 can begin
3. Tasks 1 and 2 must be completed before Task 4 can begin

Help your team when needed
As the team lead, it's your job to help and guide your team. They are supporting you, but you are also there to support them when needed. Check in with them to see how they're doing, offer help to resolve any issues they might have.

Listen to your team's ideas
Encourage your team to share their thoughts and opinions. They might have cool ideas or suggestions that can make your quinceañera even better. Working together is the key to a successful party and your team will feel like they have made tangible contributions to its success.

Celebrate your team's hard work
Say thank you often and celebrate the hard work and achievements of your dream team. This shows you respect and appreciate their contributions and keeps everyone excited about working toward your big day.

Communication and Collaboration

Planning a quinceañera is a complex process that involves working closely with many people. To create a supportive and productive environment, it's important to establish open lines of communication and promote collaboration. Here are some tips to help you foster effective communication and collaboration as you plan your big day:

Be clear and concise
When expressing your ideas, preferences, and expectations, be as clear and concise as possible. This will help avoid misunderstandings and ensure everyone is on the same page.

Listen actively
Communication is a two-way street, so make sure to listen actively to the input and suggestions of your team members. They may have valuable insights or ideas that can enhance your celebration.

Be open-minded and flexible
While it's essential to have a vision for your quinceañera, remember that things may not always go according to plan. Be open to new ideas and willing to adapt when needed.

Establish regular check-ins
Schedule regular meetings or check-ins with your team members to discuss progress, address any concerns, and ensure everyone is on track with their responsibilities.

Use technology to your advantage
Utilize group chats, shared calendars, and project management apps to streamline communication and keep everyone in the loop.

Ask how people prefer to be contacted
With so many different ways to get in touch with people these days, it doesn't hurt to ask how someone prefers to hear from you, whether it's via email, text, or a phone call.

Encourage feedback
Welcome constructive feedback from your team and be open to

making adjustments based on their input. This will help create a more collaborative environment and result in a better overall experience for everyone involved.

Show appreciation

Don't forget to express gratitude to your team members for their hard work and dedication. A simple "thank you" or "I appreciate you" can go a long way in fostering positive relationships and maintaining morale.

Tools to Keep Your Plans on Track

Being organized is essential when planning your quinceañera. Luckily, there are plenty of tools to help you stay on top of everything.

In this section, we'll explore some popular tools that can make planning your big day easier and more fun for you and your dream team.

Notebooks and Planners

A good old-fashioned planner or notebook can be your best friend when it comes to staying organized. Dedicate a special planner or notebook just for your quinceañera, where you can jot down your ideas, plans, due dates, and important contacts all in one place. A planner like Oh Happy Day's "The Essential Quinceañera Planner" has worksheets specially designed to help track and manage quinceañera planning activities.

Calendars

You can use a paper calendar, or any number of digital calendars like Google Calendar, iCal, or Outlook to keep track of appointments, meetings, and deadlines. You can even share your calendar with your team so everyone knows what's happening and when.

Task Management Apps
Apps like Trello, Asana, and Todoist can help you create to-do lists, set reminders, and assign tasks to your dream team. These apps are user-friendly and can be accessed on your phone or computer, making it easy to stay organized wherever you go.

Inspiration Boards
Use websites like Pinterest or create a physical inspiration board to collect and organize your ideas for themes, decorations, outfits, and more. This will help you visualize your quinceañera and make sure everything comes together perfectly.

Group Chat
Create a group chat on a messaging app for your team. This way, you can all communicate easily, share updates, and stay in the loop.

Kanban boards
Kanban boards are a fantastic visual tool designed to help you organize and prioritize tasks, track progress, and collaborate with your team. They give you a clear view of what needs to be done and how far along each task is.

A kanban board is typically divided into columns, each representing a stage in the task completion process. They will include columns like, "To-Do," "In Progress," and "Done". Tasks are written on cards and assigned to people. You can see the task progress as it moves from left to right.

Using a kanban board for your quinceañera can help you stay organized, work more efficiently, and ensure that nothing falls through the cracks. Plus, it's a fun and interactive way to involve your team and make sure everyone is on the same page.

There are free digital options for kanban boards. Many paid versions, like Trello and Asana, offer free versions too. You can use free versions of whiteboarding software like Miro and Mural to create kanban boards as well.

But you don't need any special software to create a kanban board. You can easily make one yourself by drawing it in a notebook, or on a whiteboard, with some sticky notes.

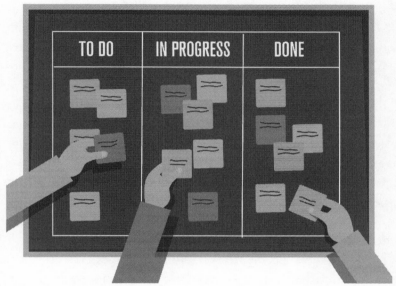

A kanban board

Managing Your Mindset

Let's face it, planning a quinceañera can be stressful and overwhelming at times. You're creating a vision of your big day, finding a dress, looking for decorations, dealing with family dynamics, and maybe there's friend drama too. Plus, you're a teenager, and your hormones are doing a number on your mind and body. It's... a lot.

It's completely natural to feel a range of emotions during the process. However, how you handle these emotions can have a significant impact on your overall experience. Remember, you can't control what other people do, only your reaction to it. In this section, we'll explore ways to manage your mindset, deal with big feelings, and navigate challenges that may arise.

First and foremost, it's essential to acknowledge and accept your emotions. It's okay to feel overwhelmed or disappointed at times, and it's important not to suppress these feelings. Instead, try to identify the cause of your emotions. If you find your emotions coming to a head, take a moment, breathe, and then collect your thoughts. You can be heard more easily if you can articulate what you are experiencing from a calm place. You might try talking to a trusted friend or family member, journaling, or practicing mindfulness techniques like meditation or deep breathing exercises.

Remember, setbacks and disappointments are a natural part of any journey. Plans fall through, people make mistakes, you may not see eye-to-eye with someone else, and miscommunications happen. It's important to approach these situations with a level head and a willingness to listen and understand both yourself and others.

Adopt a problem-solving mindset

When faced with a problem or a disagreement, it can be easy to become frustrated, emotional, or even shut down entirely. However, taking a step back and approaching the situation with a calm, clear mind can make a world of difference.

One of the keys to problem-solving is to break the issue down into manageable parts. Take some time to identify the root cause of the problem and consider what steps you can take to address it. Sometimes, it can be helpful to write down the different possible solutions and weigh the pros and cons of each. Remember that there may not be a perfect solution, but finding a workable compromise can still be a great success.

Conflict resolution can be trickier, as emotions can run high in a disagreement. One important aspect is learning to listen actively so that both parties feel heard and understood. Try to stay calm and avoid attacking or blaming the other person. Instead, focus on your own feelings and needs and try to find a way to meet both your needs and theirs. If you're struggling to find a solution, don't be afraid to bring in a neutral third party, like a mediator or counselor, to help facilitate the conversation.

While it may be challenging to face obstacles at the time, try to reframe them as opportunities for growth and learning. By staying positive, adaptable, and proactive, you can overcome any challenge and emerge stronger and more confident than before. Ultimately, developing and practicing these skills can help you to navigate any challenges that come your way with grace and confidence, and will serve you well throughout your life.

Practice relaxation techniques

Planning a big event and being in the spotlight can be stressful for anyone. Even people who perform under pressure regularly like athletes, actors, and musicians, experience anxiety leading up to and during a performance. Many have strategies and techniques they rely on to stay focused and in the moment. Grace under pressure is a skill, like any other, that you must practice to get good at it.

Here are a few approaches that you can turn to when the pressure is on:

- **Breathing exercises:** Deep, slow breathing can help calm nerves and regulate the heart rate.

- **Visualization:** Some people visualize themselves succeeding in their performance or big moment, imagining themselves executing everything perfectly.

- **Positive self-talk:** Positive affirmations can help replace negative thoughts with positive ones, creating a more confident mindset.

- **Physical relaxation:** Progressive muscle relaxation, yoga, or stretching can help reduce tension in the body.

- **Reframing thoughts:** Changing the way you think about the situation can help reduce anxiety. Instead of seeing something as an insurmountable obstacle, you can reframe it as an opportunity to practice and showcase your skills. You can transform feelings of nervousness into feelings of anticipation and excitement.

- **Cultivating gratitude:** Focusing on the present moment and being grateful for the opportunity can help shift the focus away from anxiety.

- **Rehearsal and preparation:** Adequate preparation and rehearsal can really help build confidence and reduce anxiety on stage

- **Talk to someone:** It's important to choose someone who will listen without judging you and who can offer support and encouragement. Sometimes just talking about your worries and concerns can help to alleviate some of the pressure you feel. They may be able to provide you with helpful advice or simply be a listening ear.

Scenarios

Let's look at a few scenarios and illustrate how you might approach responding to them with a productive mindset. You can also ask a friend or someone you trust if they can role-play with you to give you practice in handling a challenging situation:

Scenario 1
You had a close friend in mind to be one of your damas, but when you asked her, she declined. You may feel disappointed and hurt, but it's important to remember that people have their own reasons for saying no that may have nothing to do with you. They might

be going through their own challenges that you don't know about, they might not be able to afford to participate but might be too embarrassed to say so. Try to stay positive and respectful in your response.

You could say something like, "I understand you're unable to participate, but I want you to know that I value our friendship and appreciate your letting me know. I hope we can still have a great time at my quinceañera together." By expressing gratitude and understanding, you're showing that your friendship means more to you than any disappointment about her being one of your damas.

Remember that there are plenty of other people who would be honored to be a part of your court, so don't dwell on this one rejection. You could also take this as an opportunity to strengthen your relationship with your friend in other ways, outside of the quince.

Scenario 2

You and your mother have different opinions about the music selection for your quinceañera. Your mother prefers traditional music while you want to incorporate some hip-hop songs you and your friends enjoy.

Here's how you could approach the situation:

"Mom, I really appreciate your input on the music selection for my quinceañera, and I think having traditional music would be a wonderful way to honor my heritage, and I definitely want to include it, but I was hoping to also play some hip-hop songs that my friends and I really like. Can we work together to find a compromise that includes a mix of traditional music and hip-hop?"

You could suggest that you both make a list of songs that you like and then try to find common ground. It's important to approach the conversation with a respectful and open-minded attitude and to emphasize that you value your mother's opinion while also asserting your own preferences.

Scenario 3

A week before your event, you receive a call from the DJ you hired, and they inform you that they will no longer be able to work your reception.

First, take a breath and acknowledge your disappointment. Ask if they can recommend any other DJs. Make sure if you have signed any contracts for their services that you are covered for the return of any deposits or fees.

Take action by calling other DJs to inquire about their availability for the date of your quinceanera. Explain the situation and ask if they can accommodate your order on such short notice.

When speaking with the new DJ, you could say something like, "My original DJ has had to cancel, but I'm hopeful that you might be able to fill in on short notice. Are you available on [the date of your quinceañera] and if so, what are my options?

By being polite and direct with the new DJ, you communicate your needs and expectations clearly and respectfully. This approach will increase the likelihood that they will try to help you out.

Scenario 4

It's the day of your quinceañera, and you're feeling super nervous about giving your speech. Your stomach is in knots, and you keep going over the words in your head, worrying that you'll forget something important or stumble over your words.

Find a quiet spot. Take a deep breath and remind yourself that you've rehearsed for this moment. You've practiced your speech many times, and you know it inside and out. You're not alone in feeling nervous, and it's perfectly normal to feel this way.

Remember all the times you've overcome challenges in the past and how good it felt when you succeeded. You can do this, and you will do it well. Focus on the message you want to share with your loved ones and speak from your heart.

CHAPTER SEVEN

Find the Perfect Location

W HETHER YOUR QUINCE IS in a ballroom, community center, backyard, or park, the site will set the tone for the
event. It's important to choose a location that fits your theme,
budget, and guest list. In this chapter, we'll look at the criteria for
choosing a church and reception venue, and ensure that the setup
and cleanup are well-coordinated. We'll also discuss transportation
options and ensure everyone arrives on time and in style.

Choosing a Church for the Ceremony

If you're planning to have a religious ceremony for your
quinceañera, consider choosing a church that holds personal significance for you and your family, such as the one you regularly
attend or one with a special family connection.

Consider the following factors in choosing the right church for
your ceremony:

Size and Capacity
Make sure the church can comfortably accommodate all your

guests. Keep in mind the seating capacity, as well as space for any additional elements like musicians, a choir, or a special altar setup.

Availability
Churches can be booked for various events, including weddings, baptisms, and other ceremonies. Be sure to inquire about the availability of your preferred date and time well in advance to secure your spot.

Rules and Regulations
Different churches may have different rules regarding decorations, attire, and photography during the ceremony. Be sure to discuss these guidelines with the church administration to ensure your plans align with their requirements.

Officiant
If you have a specific priest, pastor, deacon, or other religious leader you'd like to officiate your ceremony, confirm their availability and willingness to participate. Some churches may require that their own officiants perform the ceremony, so be sure to discuss this in advance.

Location
Consider the location of the church and the location of your reception venue. Ideally, you want to minimize travel time and distance between the two locations for the convenience of your guests.

Cost
Churches may charge a fee for hosting your quinceañera ceremony. Be sure to factor this cost into your budget and discuss any additional fees that may apply, such as donations or payments for musicians.

Selecting a Site for the Reception

The site you choose can set the tone for your entire celebration. It will be the backdrop and setting for the experience. But to help you make the right decision for your quinceañera, you'll need to consider different factors, from location and capacity to amenities, style, and cost.

Reflect on your style

Think about your personal style and the theme of your quinceañera. If you're going for a glamorous event, you might consider a ballroom or a luxurious hotel. For a more rustic feel, a barn or an outdoor park might be more fitting.

Ideas for reception sites

Here are some options where you might consider hosting an event:
- Private home or backyard
- Hotels and resorts
- Event spaces
- Restaurants or clubs
- Community centers or town halls
- Parks and gardens
- Museums or galleries
- Art studios
- Vineyards
- Beaches or lakesides
- Rooftops or terraces
- Historic homes or buildings
- Farms or barns
- Boats or yachts
- Castles or mansions
- Zoos or aquariums
- Movie theaters

- Airplane hangars
- Resorts or mountain lodges
- University campuses or halls
- Warehouses or industrial spaces

Availability
Start searching for a venue early, as popular locations can book up quickly. Be prepared to be flexible with your date if you have your heart set on a particular place.

Location
Consider the convenience of the venue for your guests. If many guests will be traveling from out of town, a venue close to hotels or with easy transportation options is ideal.

Capacity
Ensure the venue has enough capacity to comfortably fit all of your guests. Ample space is necessary for guests to move around, dance, and have a good time.

Budget
Keep your budget in mind when selecting a venue. Some venues may offer packages that include catering, decorations, and other services, which can help you save money.

Facilities and amenities
Check if the venue has all the necessary facilities, like restrooms, a kitchen for food prep, a dance floor, and a stage for entertainment. Also, consider if the venue offers any extras, like a suite for getting ready or an outdoor area that can also be used.

Seating Arrangements
It is often best to consult with the venue coordinator or event planner to ensure that the tables and chairs are arranged in a way

that maximizes the available space and ensures that guests have a good view of the main events. The DJ or band should also have a clear view of the dance floor. The type of meal you choose — a sit-down dinner or a buffet, for example — will also be a factor. Additionally, you may want to consult with your family to determine who should be seated at each table, taking into consideration family dynamics and the relationships between guests.

Accessibility

When choosing a venue, consider the accessibility for all your guests, including those with mobility issues or disabilities. Make sure the venue has ramps, elevators, or other accommodations to ensure everyone can comfortably enjoy your quinceañera.

It's also a good idea to confirm that there are accessible restrooms and parking spaces available for guests who may require them. Prioritizing accessibility will ensure that all your loved ones can join you in celebrating your special day without any obstacles.

Restrictions

Some venues may have restrictions on decorations, noise levels, or the use of outside vendors. Make sure to discuss these restrictions with the venue coordinator to ensure they align with your plans.

If you're renting a commercial space, they should already have policies in place to comply with laws and regulations and insurance for hosting groups. However, if you're using a residential property, it's important to ensure that all legal requirements are met.

Visit the venue

Schedule a visit to the venue to get a feel for the space and imagine how your quinceañera will look. It's also an excellent opportunity to ask questions and discuss your ideas with the venue coordinator

Setup and Cleanup

Planning the setup for your quinceañera involves making sure everything is in place and ready for the celebration to start. This includes the decorations, tables, chairs, and other elements that will be used during the event.

Cleanup involves ensuring that the venue is left in the same condition as before the event. Cleaning up can include removing decorations, clearing tables, and ensuring that the venue is free of any trash or debris.

Most professional venues will have standard policies around setting up and cleaning up, but if you're hosting your quinceañera on private property, like someone's backyard, you will want to get clarity and confirm with the person who is responsible for the property what their rules and expectations are.

Venue Requirements
Before planning the setup and cleanup for your quinceañera, be sure to check with your venue about any specific requirements or guidelines they may have. Some venues may have restrictions on decorations, setup times, or the use of certain materials.

Setup Schedule
Create a detailed timeline for the setup process, including when decorations, tables, chairs, and other essential elements need to be in place. Be realistic with the time needed to set up and consider any potential challenges that may arise.

Vendor Coordination
Communicate with your vendors, such as caterers, decorators, and entertainment providers, about when they can access the venue for setup. Ensure everyone is on the same page regarding arrival times, setup requirements, and any necessary equipment.

Cleanup Crew
Organize a cleanup crew to help pack up decorations, clear tables, and dispose of any trash after the event. This may be a combination of family members, friends, or hired professionals. Make sure everyone knows what needs to be done and the timeline for completing the tasks.

Rental Returns
If you've rented any items, such as tables, chairs, or linens, confirm the return process with the rental company. Designate someone to be responsible for ensuring all rented items are accounted for and returned on time.

Venue Inspection
After the cleanup is complete, do a final walk-through with a representative from the venue to ensure everything has been returned to its original state. Address any issues or damages immediately to avoid potential conflicts or additional fees.

Transportation

Whether you're looking to arrive in style or simply need a reliable way to get from point A to point B, it's important to consider your options and needs. Thinking about the size of your event, the location of your venue, your guests' needs, and your personal preferences, will help you make choices from selecting the right vehicle for your grand entrance, to arranging pickups and drop-offs.

Consider Your Theme
When selecting transportation for your quinceañera, think about how it fits with the overall theme and style of your celebration. You could consider renting a vintage car, VW van, trolley, Vespa, golf cart, pedicab, or a boat. A horse-drawn carriage may be perfect

for a fairytale-themed event, while a sleek limousine might suit a more modern and elegant affair. A party bus could be both fun and practical if you have a large entourage.

Budget

Keep your budget in mind when exploring transportation options. Research various providers in your area and compare their rates to find one that meets your needs without breaking the bank. Remember that you may need to book transportation for your court as well, so be sure to factor in those costs.

Capacity

Make sure the vehicle you choose can comfortably accommodate you, your court, and any other passengers who will be riding with you. If you have a large court, consider renting a party bus or stretch limousine to ensure everyone arrives together and in style.

Reliability

Look for a transportation provider with a solid reputation for reliability and professionalism. Read reviews, ask for recommendations from friends and family, and check with the Better Business Bureau to find a trustworthy company.

Book Early

Popular transportation options can book up quickly, especially during peak event seasons. To ensure you get the vehicle you want, start researching and booking your transportation several months in advance of your quinceañera.

Plan Your Route

Plan the route from your home to the ceremony location and then to the reception venue. Make sure to account for any potential traffic or construction delays, and have a backup plan in case of unforeseen issues.

Arrival Time

Coordinate your arrival time with your photographer, videographer, and event planner to make sure everyone is ready to capture your grand entrance. Arriving fashionably late is one thing, but you don't want to keep your guests waiting too long!

Personalize Your Ride

Add a personal touch to your transportation by decorating it with ribbons, flowers, or other accents that match your quinceañera theme and color scheme. Just be sure to check with the transportation provider about any restrictions, and always err on the side of caution that ensures the safety of yourself and your guests.

Lodging & Accommodations

If you have guests visiting from out of town, you may want to recommend lodging options that are conveniently located to the venue and other local attractions. Options include hotels, resorts, motels, and vacation rentals. Each option has its pros and cons, so it's important to consider factors like cost and location, and amenities such as room size, number of beds, Wi-Fi availability, pool access, fitness center, and complimentary breakfast.

Make reservations early and take advantage of deals and discounts to save money. Many hotels offer the option of reserving a block of rooms for an event. This way, you can ensure that all of your guests have a place to stay at the same hotel and potentially even receive a group discount. It's important to reserve well in advance to ensure availability and to communicate the details to your guests so they can make their reservations on time.

Chapter Eight

Guest Lists & Communication

I N THIS CHAPTER, WE'LL talk about the heart of your quinceañera: your guests! These are all the family members, friends, and loved ones who will be there to celebrate with you.

We'll help you craft the perfect guest list and give you guidance on how to communicate with them, from creating invitations that will get everyone excited for your big day, to making a website, managing RSVPs, and making sure your thank-you notes leave a lasting impression.

We'll also cover options for going paperless and using social media. Whatever method you choose, we'll help you get out the message and make sure that your guest communication etiquette is on point.

The Guest List

One big part of planning your quince is deciding whom to invite. Carefully consider the people you'd like to share this special day with. You can use the following criteria to craft a guest list that reflects the people you would most like to celebrate your quinceañera with you:

Start with the Must-Haves
Begin by listing the people you absolutely want to attend your quince. These are the people who have been a significant part of your life and whom you couldn't imagine celebrating without.

Expand to the Nice-to-Haves
Once you've listed your must-have guests, it's time to expand your guest list to include extended family, friends, neighbors, and other acquaintances. Consider classmates, teammates, or people from your church or community groups. This is your chance to include anyone you'd like to share your special day with but keep in mind that your guest list will influence the size and budget of your celebration.

Determine Your Guest List Size and Venue Capacity
Now that you have an idea of who you'd like to invite, it's important to determine the size of your guest list and ensure that your chosen venue can accommodate everyone. Keep in mind that not all guests may be able to attend, so it's wise to invite a few more people than you expect. However, be cautious not to over-invite, as you don't want to end up with too many attendees for your venue to handle.

Consider Your Budget
Your budget will play a significant role in determining the size of your guest list. Remember that each additional guest will increase the cost of food, beverages, and other expenses. Be realistic about how many people you can afford to invite and prioritize the guests who matter most to you.

Make Adjustments

As you finalize your guest list, you may need to make some adjustments. If you find that you've invited too many people or that certain guests can't attend, it's okay to make changes. This is a normal part of the planning process, and it's essential to be flexible and adaptable.

Get Input

Your parents, madrinas, and padrinos will likely have their own ideas about who should be invited to your quinceañera. Be sure to include them in the process, as they may have valuable input and suggestions.

Invitations and Save-the-Dates

Your quinceañera invitations are the first impression your guests will have of your celebration, so it's important to make them special and make sure they are sent out in a timely fashion.

Getting the Word Out Early

Save-the-dates are typically sent out 4-6 months before the event to give your guests a heads up before sending out the formal invitations. Save-the-dates provide essential information such as the date, location, and a note that a formal invitation will follow. You can choose from various formats, such as postcards, magnets, or even digital save-the-dates sent through email or social media.

Invitation Design

When it comes to designing your quinceañera invitations, there are many options. Here are some tips for creating invitations that sparkle:

- **Choose a theme**: Your invitations should reflect the overall theme or style of your quince. Whether you're going for a glamorous, elegant, or whimsical look, your invitations should set the tone for your celebration.

- **Pick the perfect colors**: Choose colors that complement your quinceañera theme and personal style. You can use a single color or a combination of shades for a more vibrant look.

- **Select high-quality materials**: Invest in good-quality paper or cardstock for your invitations. This will make them look and feel more luxurious.

- **Work with a professional**: If you're unsure about designing your invitations, consider hiring a professional graphic designer or working with a stationery company. They can help bring your vision to life and ensure your invitations look polished and professional.

- **Buy a pre-designed template**: There are many beautiful, professionally-designed options available on marketplaces like Etsy that will allow you to find a design you like and customize the wording using an online editor.

Calligraphy

If you want to make your invitations truly stand out, hiring a professional calligrapher is a wonderful option. A calligrapher can create elegant and unique handwritten addresses and even embellish your invitations with artistic flourishes. While this option can be expensive, it adds an extra level of sophistication and personalization.

Before hiring a calligrapher, ask to see samples of their work and ensure their style aligns with your vision. Keep in mind that calligraphy will require extra time, so plan accordingly to ensure your invitations are sent out on schedule.

Mailing Your Invitations

Once your invitations are designed and printed or hand-lettered it's time to send them out. Here are some guidelines for mailing your quinceañera invitations:

Timing
Aim to send your invitations 6-8 weeks before your quinceañera. This gives your guests plenty of time to RSVP and make any necessary travel arrangements.

Addressing
Make sure to address your invitations correctly, using formal titles and full names. Double-check your guest list to ensure you have the correct addresses for all invitees. Some common titles include:

- **Mr.**: used for adult men
- **Mrs.**: used for married women
- **Ms.**: used for adult women regardless of marital status
- **Mx.**: used as a gender-neutral title
- **Miss**: used for girls and young unmarried women
- **Dr.**: used for medical doctors, dentists, and professionals with doctoral degrees
- **Prof.**: used for university professors
- **Rev.**: used for ordained ministers and clergy members
- **The Honorable** or **Judge**: used for judges

Postage
The United States Postal Service (USPS) offers a variety of stamp designs for different occasions and themes, making it easy to add a personal touch to your mail.

Some stamp themes that would work well for a quinceañera might be heart, floral, and nature-themed stamps. One popular series of stamps is the "Forever" series, which features a variety of designs and themes and can be used to mail a one-ounce letter no matter how much the cost of postage may rise in the future.

Finally, don't forget to weigh your invitations and include the proper postage. If you're using any embellishments, such as ribbons or wax seals, keep in mind that these may require additional postage.

RSVPs

Include an RSVP card with a self-addressed, stamped envelope for guests to easily respond. Set an RSVP deadline, typically 3-4 weeks before the event, to give you enough time to finalize your guest count and make any necessary arrangements. You may also want to give your guests the option to contact you via email on the RSVP.

By following these tips, you'll create save-the-dates and invitations that not only stand out but also effectively communicate the excitement and importance of your quince. Remember, your invitations are the first glimpse your guests will have of your special day, so make them memorable and personal!

Other Printed Materials

Printed materials are not limited to just invitations. There may be other printed matter that provides helpful information to your guests that you'd like to include, including:

- Programs
- Seating Chart
- Menus
- Place cards
- Name cards
- Directional signage (e.g., signage that helps guests navigate the reception site, including where restrooms or changing rooms are)

These small touches and personalizations can really help your guests feel included and special, but they do require forethought and planning, so if you plan to incorporate these things, be sure you have accounted for them in your timeline and budget.

Bear in mind that all your printed materials should also have the same look and feel as your quinceañera theme so that when you look at all the printed pieces together they appear to be from the same event.

Going Paperless

Paperless communication is a great option that can also be eco-friendly, cost-effective, and convenient. From invitations to directions and everything in between, there are a variety of paperless options available to help you communicate with your guests.

There are many free and paid online invitation services, like Evite, Paperless Post, and Greenvelope, that offer customizable templates for digital invitations that can be easily personalized with your event details. You can then send these invitations via email or through social media platforms, and many also offer features like tracking RSVPs. Not only is this option more environmentally friendly, but it can also save you money on printing and postage costs.

You can also use online maps to provide easy-to-follow directions and other important details for your guests. Create a map with important locations, including the site of the ceremony, reception, and lodging.

Another paperless option is to create a website. Your website can include all the details about your event, such as the date, time, location, and dress code. You can provide helpful details like phone numbers for transportation services, and your contact information. Your website can include program information about the activities that will be happening throughout the evening.

By providing all the information in one place, your guests can easily access all the details they need to know. But be mindful that designing a website takes skill and not everyone will find a website an easy way to get the information they need. A website may just be one method you use to communicate with your guests. For more guidance on creating a website, please see the chapter, "Websites & Social Media."

Finally, keep in mind that websites and digital correspondence may not last forever. If you want to have something physically tangible you can hold on to as a keepsake of your day, you may want to consider going the traditional paper route. You might also do a combination of digital and paper communications to accommodate a variety of needs and preferences.

Managing RSVPs

Keeping track of RSVPs is crucial for the smooth planning of your quinceañera. By effectively managing your RSVPs, you can ensure that your quinceañera runs smoothly and that you have an accurate headcount for your venue, catering, and other event arrangements.

Here are some tips to help you manage your RSVPs effectively:

- **Set a Clear Deadline**: When sending out your invitations, be sure to include a clear RSVP deadline. This gives your guests a timeline and helps you finalize the headcount for your event.

- **Provide Multiple RSVP Options**: Make it easy for your guests to respond by offering multiple options for RSVPs, such as email, phone, or even a response card included with the invitation.

- **Use a Tracking System**: Keep a list or spreadsheet to track the RSVPs as they come in. This will help you stay organized and make it easier to follow up with guests who haven't responded.

- **Send Gentle Reminders**: As the RSVP deadline approaches, send a friendly reminder to those who haven't responded yet. A simple text message or phone call can make a difference in getting a timely response.

- **Be Prepared for Last-Minute Changes**: Even with the best planning, there may be last-minute changes or cancellations. Be flexible and prepared to adjust your plans accordingly.

Thank You Etiquette

In today's fast-paced, digital world, handwritten thank-you notes might seem a bit old-fashioned, but they still hold great importance in acknowledging a person's gift and showing gratitude. There's no substitute for a personal, handwritten note, as it demonstrates that you took the time and effort to express your appreciation sincerely.

With our inboxes overflowing with emails and our phones buzzing with text messages, a handwritten thank you note stands out as a thoughtful gesture that won't go unnoticed. It's a genuine way to connect with people and show them that their gift or presence at your celebration meant a lot to you.

Practicing good manners helps you build stronger relationships with friends and family, fosters a positive image of you in the minds of others, and encourages an atmosphere of kindness and appreciation. So, even if it seems a bit old-fashioned, never underestimate the power of a heartfelt thank-you note – it's a small gesture that goes a long way.

Thank You Cards
You can save time and ensure a consistent design by ordering thank-you cards along with your save-the-dates and invitations.

This way, you'll have them ready to go once the event is over. Don't forget to purchase postage in advance too.

If you prefer to use images from your celebration on your thank you cards, you can wait until after your quinceañera to purchase them. This allows you to choose your favorite photos and create a personalized, memorable keepsake for your guests. Online companies like Shutterfly, Moo, and Snapfish, and stores like CVS, Walgreens, and Walmart, offer customizable thank you cards with photo options.

Be sure to personalize each thank you note by mentioning the specific gift the guest gave you and any special moments you shared with them during the celebration. This will make the note more heartfelt and memorable.

Remember, the most important thing is to express your gratitude to your guests promptly. Aim to send your thank you cards within a month of your quinceañera to make sure your guests know how much their presence and gifts meant to you.

Thank You Note Examples
Here are a few examples of thank you notes you can write to express your gratitude for the gifts and/or presence of your guests at your quinceañera:

Example 1
Dear [Guest's Name],

I wanted to thank you so much for coming to my quinceañera and for the lovely [gift name]. Your presence made the day even more special, and I truly appreciate the time and effort you took to celebrate with me. I'll cherish the [gift name] and remember the wonderful memories we shared on my special day.

Thank you once again!

Love,

[Your Name]

Example 2

Hi [Guest's Name],

I can't thank you enough for attending my quinceañera and for the amazing [gift name]! I was so excited to see you there, and your gift was just perfect. Every time I use it, I'll think of you and the fun we had at my party.

Your support means the world to me!

Hugs,

[Your Name]

Example 3

Dear [Guest's Name],

I hope this note finds you well! I just wanted to thank you for coming to my quinceañera and for the beautiful [gift name]. Your thoughtfulness and generosity truly warmed my heart. I had a wonderful time, and I hope you did too.

Thank you for being a part of my special day!

With love,

[Your Name]

Chapter Nine

Menu Planning

N O QUINCEAÑERA IS COMPLETE without delicious food! Food can be a conversation starter, encouraging guests to mingle, share stories, and create connections. In planning your menu, consider the preferences and dietary needs of your guests to ensure that everyone feels welcome and included.

Selecting a Theme

The first thing you need to do is determine the overall theme and feel of your celebration, the number of guests, and the venue or site. For example, a garden party with 30 people in a backyard or a black-tie gala with 200 people in a ballroom.

Your menu should reflect your theme. If you're having a garden party, you might want to include fresh, seasonal ingredients and light dishes, while a winter wonderland theme might call for more hearty and warming options.

Meal Styles

Once you have a clear idea of these factors, you can consider different meal styles that would best suit your event.

Buffet
If you want a more relaxed and informal vibe, a buffet-style meal might be the way to go. This allows guests to pick and choose what they want to eat and mingle with others while they eat. Buffets are also generally less expensive than other options and can be a good choice if you're working within a tight budget.

Sit-Down
For a more formal and elegant affair, a sit-down meal is a traditional choice. This style of meal allows for a more structured timeline, as each course is served in succession. However, it can be more expensive and may limit guests' food choices.

Family-Style
Family-style dining is a mix of the two styles. In this style, platters of food are placed on each table, and guests serve themselves. This is a great way to encourage guests to interact with one another and allows for a more casual atmosphere.

Food Preferences

Start by thinking about your food preferences, favorite dishes, and flavors. Are there any cultural or family recipes that hold a special place in your heart? Try to include foods that you love and represent you in some way. Keep in mind the preferences and dietary restrictions of your guests. It's a good idea to have options for vegetarians, vegans, and people with allergies or intolerances, such as gluten-free or nut-free dishes.

Selecting a Caterer

Ask for recommendations from friends and family, read reviews, and schedule tastings with a few top choices. Make sure to discuss your preferences, theme, and any dietary restrictions with the caterer to ensure they can accommodate your needs.

Work with your chosen caterer to finalize your menu, making sure it includes a variety of options, such as appetizers, main courses, and desserts. Don't forget to plan for late-night snacks or food stations to keep guests satisfied throughout the celebration.

Sample Menus

These menus show you examples of how creative you can be in designing a menu. You might choose to go the traditional route, or showcase a completely different type of cuisine that complements your theme.

LATIN AMERICAN MENUS
These menus offer a mix of classic Latin American dishes as well as fusion flavors

Traditional Mexican Feast
Appetizers:
• Guacamole and chips
• Mini chicken taquitos
• Elote (Mexican street corn)

Main Course:
• Chicken enchiladas with red sauce
• Carne asada (grilled steak)
• Chile relleno (stuffed poblano peppers)

Sides:
• Spanish rice
• Refried beans
• Mixed green salad with avocado dressing

Dessert:
• Tres leches cake
• Churros with chocolate dipping sauce

Beverages:
• Horchata (rice milk drink)
• Agua de Jamaica (hibiscus tea)
• Sparkling water

Caribbean Delight
Appetizers:
• Empanadas (stuffed pastries)
• Tostones (fried plantains) with garlic dipping sauce
• Ceviche with mango and avocado

Main Course:
• Ropa vieja (shredded beef in tomato sauce)
• Arroz con pollo (chicken with rice)
• Grilled fish with mango salsa

Sides:
• Black beans and rice
• Caribbean coleslaw with pineapple
• Fried yuca with garlic-cilantro sauce

Dessert:
• Flan de coco (coconut flan)
• Pastelillos de guayaba (guava pastries)

Beverages:
- Virgin piña coladas
- Batido de trigo (Cuban milkshake)
- Horchata de ajonjolí (sesame horchata)

South American Fusion
Appetizers:
- Causa limeña (Peruvian potato salad)
- Tequeños (Venezuelan cheese sticks)
- Salpicón de mariscos (seafood salad)

Main Course:
- Lomo saltado (Peruvian stir-fried beef)
- Aji de gallina (Peruvian creamy chicken)
- Vegetarian quinoa-stuffed peppers

Sides:
- White rice
- Yuca al mojo (cassava with garlic sauce)
- Ensalada rusa (South American-style potato salad)

Dessert:
- Alfajores (dulce de leche sandwich cookies)
- Pastel de tres leches (three milk cake)

Beverages:
- Chicha morada (Peruvian purple corn drink)
- Guanabana juice
- Lemon-lime soda

THEMED MENUS
These fun and imaginative theme menus will add a touch of whimsy and excitement to your quinceañera, taking your guests on a culinary journey through different settings and styles. A menu

that complements your theme, and coordinating decorations and table settings will create a truly immersive experience.

Hollywood Glamour
Appetizers:
• Caprese skewers with balsamic glaze
• Crab-stuffed mushrooms
• Prosciutto-wrapped asparagus

Main Course:
• Chicken Marsala
• Grilled salmon with lemon herb butter
• Truffle risotto with roasted mushrooms and asparagus

Sides:
• Garlic mashed potatoes
• Grilled vegetable medley
• Caesar salad with homemade croutons

Dessert:
• Chocolate fondue with assorted fruit and marshmallows
• Mini fruit tarts

Beverages:
• Cranberry Spritzers
• Arnold Palmers
• Fruit-infused water

Enchanted Forest Theme
Appetizers:
• Stuffed mushroom caps with goat cheese and herbs
• Mini quiches with spinach and feta
• Prosciutto and melon bites

Main Course:
- Herb-crusted roast beef with a red wine sauce
- Grilled chicken with mushroom sauce
- Vegetable and ricotta stuffed shells

Sides:
- Rosemary roasted potatoes
- Green beans almondine
- Mixed green salad with candied walnuts and cranberries

Dessert:
- Forest berry tartlets
- Chocolate mousse cups

Beverages:
- Elderflower and cucumber mocktails
- Lavender lemonade
- Sparkling water with fresh fruit garnishes

Carnival Theme
Appetizers:
- Mini corn dogs with mustard and ketchup
- Soft pretzel bites with cheese sauce
- Popcorn shrimp with cocktail sauce

Main Course:
- Gourmet burgers with assorted toppings
- Grilled hot dogs with a variety of condiments
- Pulled pork sliders with coleslaw

Sides:
- Macaroni and cheese
- Potato salad
- Grilled corn on the cob

Dessert:
- Funnel cake with powdered sugar and fruit toppings
- Cotton candy

Beverages:
- Classic root beer floats
- Freshly squeezed lemonade
- Iced tea with mint

Designing Your Dream Cake

Your quinceañera cake is not only a delicious treat to be enjoyed by your guests, but it's also a stunning centerpiece that reflects your personality and style.

Designing your dream cake requires thought, creativity, and careful planning. It serves as a focal point for the reception when everyone comes together to commemorate this milestone and also serves as an opportunity for memorable photos.

The following steps will help you navigate the process and ensure that your cake is the centerpiece of your reception:

- **Cake Consultation**: Begin by scheduling a consultation with a professional cake designer or a reputable bakery. During the consultation, discuss your vision, theme, and preferred flavors. Bring along pictures of cakes that inspire you, color swatches to match your theme, and any other relevant details.

- **Choose Your Flavors**: Quinceañera cakes often have multiple tiers, which means you can choose different flavors for each layer. Consider offering a variety of flavors to please your guests' diverse tastes. Popular options include vanilla, chocolate, red velvet, lemon, and carrot

cake. Don't forget about the fillings, such as fruit pre-
serves, chocolate ganache, or flavored buttercream.

* **Size and Structure**: The size of your cake will depend on
  the number of guests attending your quinceañera. Your
  cake designer will help you determine the appropriate
  number of tiers and servings. If you're dreaming of a
  towering cake but don't have a large guest list, consider
  adding faux tiers for visual impact without wasting cake
  and incurring unnecessary expenses.

* **Cake Design**: Your cake should reflect the theme and
  style of your quinceañera. If you have a specific design
  in mind, share it with your cake designer. They can help
  you refine your ideas and bring your vision to life. Popular
  design elements include flowers, lace patterns, fondant
  bows, and monograms. Don't be afraid to get creative and
  think outside the box.

* **Cake Topper**: A beautiful cake topper can add a personal
  touch to your cake. Traditional quinceañera toppers may
  include a figurine of the birthday girl in her gown, a tiara,
  or the number "15." Alternatively, you can choose something unique, such as a custom-made topper featuring
  your name or initials, or something that symbolizes your
  hobbies, interests, or heritage.

* **Cake Delivery and Setup**: Arrange for your cake to be
  delivered to the venue on the day of your quinceañera.
  Coordinate with the venue staff and your cake designer to
  ensure the cake is set up in a prominent location, where
  it can be admired by your guests. Don't forget to have
  a designated cake-cutting area with a cake stand, cutting
  utensils, and plates.

Preserving the Memories
Keep in mind that the cake will be a focal point for photographs and memories. Be sure to capture the cake in all its glory before it's cut and served. If you're working with a professional photographer be sure to add this to your shot list.

Cake Alternatives
There are plenty of fun and whimsical alternatives to a traditional cake that can be showstoppers in their own right. With a few props and presentation tricks, this can be an economical, delectable, and spectacular approach.

Here are some cake alternatives to get your creativity flowing. You can find many stunning and delectable examples on Pinterest and Instagram for inspiration:

• Macaron Tower
• Doughnut Tower
• Brownie Stack
• Cupcake Tower
• Profiteroles Stack
• Croquembouche
• Mille Crêpes
• Rice Crispy Tower
• Chocolate Strawberry Tower
• Cake Pops Tower
• Meringue Kisses Tower
• Tower of Waffles
• Dessert Bar
• Churro Bar
• Ice Cream Bar
• Chocolate Fountain

CHAPTER TEN

Dresses & Attire

THE QUINCEAÑERA DRESS IS a symbol of elegance and grace. With all eyes on you on your big day, you want to look and feel like a star. Your court will also need to look sharp and complement you beautifully as well.

In this chapter we'll guide you through the process of selecting your dress, your court's attire, and dance outfits. We'll also talk shoes, accessories, hair, and makeup. Finally, we'll discuss the importance of self-care, ensuring you feel radiant and grounded.

Whatever your style, let your true self shine through as you put together the perfect dress, accessories, and makeup into a stunning ensemble that will make you feel confident and beautiful from head to toe, inside and out.

Selecting the Perfect Dress

Selecting the perfect quinceañera dress is one of the most important parts of the planning process. Remember to start early, establish your budget, do your research, choose a style that you feel good in, select accessories, and budget time and money for alterations. With these tips in mind, you'll be sure to find a dress that makes you feel confident, beautiful, and ready for your special day.

Begin Early
One of the most important things to keep in mind when it comes to selecting your quinceañera dress is to start early. This will give you plenty of time to find the perfect dress that fits both your style and budget. Waiting until the last minute could limit your options and add unnecessary stress to an already busy time. Ideally, you should begin the dress search process about 8-10 months before your quinceañera. This will give you enough time to browse different styles, try on dresses, make alterations, and plan for accessories.

Establish Your Budget
It's crucial to establish your budget early on. Determine how much money you're able and willing to spend on your dress and factor in any additional costs such as alterations, accessories, and shoes. Be realistic about what you can afford and stick to your budget to avoid overspending. Keep in mind that your dress is just one aspect of your quinceañera celebration, and there are many other expenses to consider.

Conduct Your Research
Before you start shopping for your quinceañera dress, it's important to do your research. Browse online to get an idea of the different styles and colors that are available, and make note of the dresses that catch your eye. Consider the style of your party and what type of dress would fit best with the theme. Look for inspiration in magazines, online, and in real life by attending bridal expos, quinceañera events, or even window shopping at local dress stores. You can also ask friends, family, and your event planner for recommendations on where to shop.

Choosing the Style

Once you have a general idea of the style and color you want, it's time to start trying on dresses. Focus on finding a dress that makes you feel confident and beautiful. Consider the length of the dress as well, which can range from short and flirty to long and elegant.

Some common styles of quinceañera dresses include ball gowns, A-line dresses, and mermaid dresses. Ball gowns are a classic choice for quinceañeras and feature a full, voluminous skirt and fitted bodice. A-line dresses have a fitted bodice that flares out slightly at the waist, creating an "A" shape. This style is universally flattering and can be dressed up or down depending on the occasion. Mermaid dresses are fitted through the bodice and hips and flare out at the knees, creating a dramatic silhouette.

When it comes to choosing the length of your dress, you can opt for a traditional long gown or go for something shorter and more modern. If you're having a formal quinceañera, a long gown is usually the way to go. However, if you're having a more casual or contemporary celebration, a shorter dress can be a fun and stylish option.

Finally, it's important to consider the color of your dress. Traditionally, quinceañera dresses are white or pink, but there are no hard and fast rules when it comes to color. Some girls opt for bold, bright colors like red or blue, while others prefer softer shades like lavender or mint green. Ultimately, the color you choose should make you feel confident and beautiful on your special day.

There are several styles of dresses to choose from when it comes to quinceañera dresses. Here are some of the most popular styles:

- **Ballgown**: This is the most traditional and classic style for a quinceañera dress. Ballgowns typically have a fitted bodice and a full, voluminous skirt that extends to the floor. They can be made with a variety of materials, such as tulle, organza, or lace, and often feature intricate embellishments such as beading or embroidery.

- **A-line**: A-line dresses are a popular choice for quinceañera dresses because they are universally flattering. These dresses have a fitted bodice and a skirt that flares out in an A shape. They are often made with lightweight fabrics such as chiffon or silk and can be adorned with lace, beading, or other decorative elements.

- **Mermaid**: Mermaid dresses are form-fitting through the bodice and hips and then flare out at the bottom, resembling a mermaid's tail. This style is often made with stretchy fabrics like jersey or spandex and can be adorned with lace, sequins, or other embellishments.

- **Two-piece**: Two-piece dresses are a more modern and unique option for a quinceañera dress. These dresses consist of a separate top, or corset, and skirt that can be mixed and matched to create a customized look. The top can range from a crop top to a long-sleeved blouse, and the skirt can be a full ballgown or a sleek, fitted style. The advantage of a two-piece is that while it can be designed to look like one gown it is also easier to get into and out of for quick wardrobe changes, such as for the surprise dance.

- **High-low**: High-low dresses are a fun and flirty option for a quinceañera dress. These dresses have a shorter front hemline that gradually lengthens towards the back, creating a unique and eye-catching silhouette. High-low dresses can be made with a variety of fabrics, and often feature decorative elements like ruffles or lace.

- **Column**: A column dress is a sleek and form-fitting style that follows the natural shape of the body. The dress is typically straight and narrow, with a hemline that falls at or below the knee. The column dress is often made of a lightweight and flowing fabric, such as silk or chiffon, and can be adorned with various embellishments. This style of dress is simple and elegant, making it a popular choice for formal events and weddings.

These are just a few examples of the many styles of quinceañera dresses available. When choosing a style, it's important to consider your personal preferences, body type, and the overall theme and style of your celebration.

Alterations

Once you've found your dream dress, don't forget to budget time and money for alterations. Almost every dress will need some adjustments to fit perfectly, so plan for multiple fittings to ensure a flawless fit. Find a reputable tailor or dress shop that specializes in quinceañera dresses and make sure to communicate your needs and preferences clearly. Allow plenty of time for alterations, as they can take several weeks to complete depending on the complexity of the changes.

Shoes & Accessories

Think about the shoes, jewelry, and headpieces that will complement your dress and complete your look.

Choose accessories that match the style and color of your dress and consider practicality as well. You'll be dancing and celebrating, so choose comfortable shoes that won't hurt your feet after a few hours. A clutch or small purse is also a good idea to keep your phone, lipstick, and other essentials close at hand.

From jewelry to hair pieces, here are some tips to help you coordinate your accessories with your dress and complete your look.

Types of Accessories

Jewelry
Necklaces, bracelets, earrings, and rings are all popular choices for quinceañera jewelry. Consider the different materials and tones, such as silver, gold, rose gold, rhinestones, diamonds, and pearls, and choose pieces that complement your dress and personal style.

Hair Accessories
Tiaras, headbands, hair combs, and clips can add a special touch to your hairstyle and overall look. Consider the style and color of your dress when choosing hair accessories, and make sure they are comfortable to wear throughout the day.

Shoes
Whether you choose high heels, flats, or sneakers, your shoes should be comfortable and match your dress style and color.

Handbags
A small clutch or purse can be a practical accessory for holding your phone, lipstick, and other essentials throughout the day.

Coordinating Accessories

When coordinating your accessories, it's important to choose pieces that complement your dress without overwhelming it. Here are some tips to keep in mind:

Consider the style
If your dress has intricate details, you may want to keep your accessories more simple and understated. Alternatively, if your dress is relatively simple, you can add more sparkle and bling with your accessories.

Match metals
If your dress has gold beading or embellishments, consider choosing gold-tone jewelry and accessories to match. If your dress has silver accents, go for silver-tone pieces.

Mix and match
That said, don't be afraid to mix and match different metals and tones or add a pop of color with your jewelry or hair accessories. Just be sure to balance everything out so your overall look is cohesive and balanced.

The Tiara
The tiara is a traditional accessory and is often considered the centerpiece of the outfit. When choosing a tiara, consider the size, style, and color, and make sure it complements your dress and personal style.

Finding the Right Shoes
While it's traditional to change into high heels as part of the celebration, many quinceañeras opt for options like flats, sneakers, and even boots for the other parts of the day, that represent who they are.

Begin by considering the length and style of your dress to determine the type of shoe that would work best. For example, if you're wearing a ball gown, you may want to opt for a pair of elegant heels or flats, while a shorter dress may look better with strappy sandals or pumps.

When it comes to the color of your shoes, you have a few options. You can go for a classic and traditional look by choosing shoes that match the color of your dress or go for a contrasting color that complements your dress.

You can also choose shoes with embellishments or sparkles to add a bit of glam to your overall look. But your shoes don't have to match your dress perfectly - you can always choose a fun, contrasting color or pattern to add some personality to your look.

Comfort is key when it comes to choosing shoes for your quinceañera. Make sure to try on a variety of styles and sizes to find a pair that fits well and doesn't pinch or rub your feet. If you're not used to wearing heels, it's a good idea to break them in ahead of time to avoid discomfort or blisters. Consider bringing a backup pair of shoes in case your feet get tired during the festivities.

Lastly, don't forget about the practicality of your shoes. If you're having an outdoor celebration, stilettos may not be the best option, as they can easily sink into grass or dirt. Opt for a wedge or block heel instead, which provides stability and support on uneven surfaces.

Whatever footwear you choose, make sure it reflects your personal style and allows you to enjoy your special day to the fullest.

Court of Honor Attire

The court, consisting of the damas and chambelanes, traditionally wears matching outfits to complement the quinceañera's gown.

Often, the damas will wear matching or coordinating dresses or gowns, while the chambelanes will wear matching suits or tuxedos. The outfits can be rented or purchased, and some quinceañeras may choose to add special touches such as custom embroidery or embellishments to make the outfits unique.

It's important to plan and coordinate the court wardrobe early on in the quinceañera planning process to ensure that everyone looks cohesive and stylish on the big day.

Here are some points to consider when selecting the wardrobe for the court:

Colors
Choose a color scheme that complements the quinceañera's dress and the overall theme of the event.

Style

The style of the court's wardrobe should match the formality of the event. For example, a formal event may require tuxedos and ball gowns, while a more casual event may call for sundresses and khakis.

Coordination

Coordinate the wardrobe of the court members so that they look cohesive and complement your dress and theme. The classic solution is for them to wear matching ensembles, with all the damas in the same style and color dress, and all the chambelanes in matching suits or tuxedos.

Another option is for them to wear complementary or contrasting colors. If you're wearing a blush pink dress, the damas might wear dresses in shades of rose, mauve, or champagne. Another option is to choose a contrasting color. If you're in a light blue dress, then the damas might wear navy blue dresses.

You can also mix it up. For example, the court may be color coded with one damas in a pink dress and a chambelan with a pink bowtie, a second damas in a blue dress and a chambelan with a blue bowtie, and a third damas in a purple dress and a chambelan with a purple bowtie. Or you might choose to have the chambelanes and damas matching but your escort's attire to be different than the rest to set them apart. Experiment with different ideas and have fun with them!

Damas' Attire

Here are some considerations for the damas' attire:

Dress Length

The length of the dress should be chosen based on the style and level of formality of the event, as well as the personal preferences of the quinceañera and her family.

Short dresses are a popular choice for damas. They offer a fun and youthful look while still being appropriate for a formal event. Knee-length dresses offer a balance between casual and formal.

Floor-length dresses are popular and appropriate for more formal quinceañeras.

Tea-length or midi dresses are dresses that fall between the knee and ankle. They can have a vintage, retro feel to them, and are often seen as a happy medium between a full-length gown and a shorter dress.

Dress styles

A-line dresses are a classic choice, with a fitted bodice and a flared skirt that flatters many body types.

Fit-and-flare dresses are similar but have a more defined waistline.

Sheath dresses offer a more fitted, modern, streamlined look, while shift dresses are a looser, more relaxed style.

Empire waist dresses feature a high waistline that falls just below the bust, creating a flowy and flattering silhouette. Empire waist dresses can be long or short and are often made from lightweight fabrics like chiffon or silk.

Skirt and top sets

Skirt and top sets can be a fun and versatile option. They allow for the mixing and matching of styles and colors and can be dressed up or down depending on the quinceañera's theme. Because they are separate, you can swap out the pieces to get a different look very easily without needing a complete outfit change, which can be useful for the dances.

Jumpsuits

Jumpsuits are an unusual, modern option. They can be in a variety of colors and styles, such as off-the-shoulder or halter necklines, and can be dressed up with statement jewelry or heels. They might be a great look for a vintage, retro-themed quinceañera, or a disco surprise dance.

Shoes
The shoes should match or complement the dress and overall theme. It's important to choose shoes that are easy to walk and dance in since damas will be on their feet for a good portion of the night. Strappy sandals, pumps, flats, and wedges, are all good options.

Accessories
Accessories can add a pop of color, sparkle, or texture to a dama's dress, and they can also help to tie the outfit together. Accessories may include earrings, necklaces, bracelets, hair clips or combs, and clutches or purses. Accessories should complement the dress and not overpower it, so it's important to choose pieces that are in proportion to the dress and that add to the overall aesthetic.

Chambelanes' Attire

Here are some ideas for the chambelanes' attire:

Tuxedos
For a formal and elegant event, chambelanes can wear tuxedos with cummerbunds that coordinate with the quinceañera's gown.

Suit and tie
A classic look that is always in style, a well-tailored suit and tie is a great option for chambelanes. A navy blue or charcoal gray suit is a classic choice that can work for a variety of occasions. Black is also a formal option but can feel more somber.

When choosing a suit material, look for a wool blend for durability and wrinkle resistance. For a more modern and unique look, consider having the chambelanes wear colored suits that match the color scheme of the event. In warmer weather, khaki, seersucker, and light grey are also good options.

Themed attire

Depending on the theme of the quinceañera, the chambelanes could dress in attire that matches the theme, such as Hawaiian shirts for a luau-themed event.

Traditional cultural attire

The chambelanes can wear traditional attire such as a charro outfit or a guayabera shirt.

Military dress uniforms

If the chambelanes are members of a military organization, they could wear their dress uniforms for the event.

Shirts

A classic white dress shirt is a timeless choice that pairs well with any suit color. For a more modern twist, consider a light blue or pale pink shirt. When selecting a shirt material, stick with cotton or a cotton blend for a crisp, polished look.

Ties & Bow Ties

There are many different styles of ties, including the classic straight tie and the bow tie. A solid color tie is a safe bet for any occasion, but a pattern like stripes or dots can add visual interest.

The most common necktie knots are the four-in-hand, the half-Windsor, and the Windsor. The four-in-hand is the simplest and most versatile, while the half-Windsor and Windsor knots are larger and more formal.

For a formal event, a bow tie in black is classic. Bow ties can be pre-tied, clip-on, and self-tie.

Shoes

Black shoes are a classic choice that goes well with just about any color suit, but brown shoes can also be a versatile option depending on the shade of the suit.

For navy and dark blue suits, brown shoes in shades like cognac or chestnut can add some warmth and depth to the look.

For grey suits, black or brown shoes can work well depending on the shade of the suit. Lighter grey suits may look better with brown shoes, while darker grey suits may look better with black shoes.

Beige or khaki suits can be paired with brown or tan shoes for a casual yet sophisticated look.

It's important to keep in mind the style of the shoe as well. There are several types of shoes that pair well with suits for men, including oxfords, derbies, loafers, and monk straps.

Dress shoes with a polished finish are the most formal option, while matte finishes or textured leathers can give a more casual vibe. Suede shoes are another option for a more relaxed look, but may not be appropriate for very formal events.

Socks

The conservative approach is to match dark socks to dark trousers, and mid-calf or longer-length socks, which ensure legs remain covered even when sitting. The creative approach includes coordinating socks with different solid colors, patterns, and motifs to complement the outfit. Athletic socks should be avoided, as they lack the aesthetics required for a suit outfit.

Accessories

Accessories to consider include cufflinks, pocket squares, and boutonnieres.

Cufflinks are a great way to add a touch of sophistication and elegance to the outfit. They come in a variety of styles and materials, from simple silver or gold to more elaborate designs.

Pocket squares are a fun and playful accessory that can add a pop of color to the outfit. They can be folded in a variety of ways to create different looks.

Finally, a boutonniere is a small flower that is worn on the lapel of the jacket. It adds a touch of elegance and tradition to the outfit.

Surprise Dance Outfits

Many quinceañeras change into a different outfit for their surprise dance. Here are a few things to consider when choosing your surprise dance ensemble:

Comfort
The surprise dance usually involves a lot of movement, so it's important to choose an outfit that is comfortable and allows you to go through your steps with ease.

Style
The outfit should reflect your personality and the theme of the song.

Accessories
The right accessories can really make a surprise dance outfit stand out. Think about adding a belt, jewelry, or a unique headpiece to complete the look.

Surprise Dance Outfit Ideas

Here is inspiration for surprise dance outfits to help you spark ideas:

- **1950s-themed**: A full-skirted swing dress with a cinched waist and petticoat and saddle shoes. A scarf around your neck, and a retro updo hairstyle. For the chambelanes, a white t-shirt with rolled sleeves, and cuffed jeans for a cool James Dean-inspired look. A pair of black loafers or Converse sneakers.

- **Hip-hop-themed**: Streetwear, including graphic t-shirts, jerseys, hoodies, distressed denim jeans, and sneakers. For a sleek and minimal look, go for an all-black outfit with a simple t-shirt or tank top, black jeans, black sneakers, and a black baseball cap.

- **Western-themed**: Ruffled blouses, jeans, and cowboy boots for the quinceañera and damas. Western shirts, jeans, and cowboy boots and hats for the chambelanes.

- **Fairytale-themed**: Tutus and ballet flats for the quinceañera and damas. Suit vest and slacks for the chambelanes. If the chambelanes are wearing three-piece suits for the *vals*, they can just remove the jacket for the surprise dance.

- **Matching T-Shirts**: Custom, matching t-shirts for the court. This can be a fun and cost-effective option that adds personalization and can also serve as a keepsake for your quinceañera.

CHAPTER ELEVEN

Hair, Makeup, & Self-Care

I F THE DRESS IS the star of the quinceañera, then hair and makeup are the supporting actors that elevate the whole performance. They enhance your natural beauty, complement your dress, and make you feel confident and polished.

Beauty also comes from within, and self-care is an essential component of your overall well-being. It involves valuing and taking care of yourself, both physically and mentally, to ensure that you not only look your best but feel your best on the big day.

Hiring a professional can take some of the stress off of you, and they have the skills and experience to create the perfect look. However, doing it yourself can be more cost-effective and you have more control over the final result.

It's important to start planning your hair and makeup early. This will give you time to experiment with different hairstyles, try out different makeup looks, and make any necessary changes. It's also a good idea to have a trial run with your hairstylist and makeup artist before the big day.

Finally, throughout the day, you may need to refresh your hair and makeup to keep it looking fresh and polished. You can also ask a bridesmaid or family member to help you with touch-ups throughout the day.

Hairstyles

Don't be afraid to try out different hairstyles before settling on the final look for your quinceañera.

Do some research and find inspiration from magazines, online sources, or even from your hairstylist. You can browse social media platforms like Instagram, TikTok, and Pinterest for inspiration.

It's important to consider the style of your dress and the overall theme of your celebration when choosing your hairstyle. You want your hair to make you feel confident and beautiful.

Most hairstyles allow for a range of hair accessories to be added, such as headbands, barrettes, and ribbons, to add extra sparkle and glamour to the look.

Here are some common styles. Keep in mind that there are also variations and combinations of each style:

- **Updos**: Updos are a classic and elegant hairstyle created by pulling the hair up and back, and securing it in place with bobby pins, hair ties, or other hair accessories. Updos can vary in complexity and style, from a simple and sleek bun to an intricate braided updo with twists and curls. One of the benefits of an updo is that it keeps the hair off the neck and shoulders, and allows for the hair to be styled in a way that showcases the neckline and back of the dress, adding an extra touch of sophistication, and femininity to the overall look.

- **Classic Chignon**: This timeless updo features a low bun at the nape of the neck. It's a great choice for those who want an elegant and sophisticated look.

- **French Twist**: The French twist is a classic updo that's perfect for formal occasions. It is created by twisting the hair from the nape of the neck upward and securing it with bobby pins or hairpins to create a rolled shape that sits on top of the head. The hair is often teased at the crown to add height and volume.

- **Messy Bun**: The messy bun is a popular updo for those who want a more relaxed and casual look. It's perfect for outdoor celebrations or for those who want a more bohemian vibe.

- **Half-up, half-down hairstyles**: The half-up half-down hairstyle offers a stylish and elegant look while also being practical and comfortable. This hairstyle is achieved by pulling back the top half of the hair and securing it with a hair tie or clip while leaving the bottom half loose and flowing. It can be dressed up or down depending on the occasion, and it complements most face shapes and hair textures.

- **Braided hairstyles**: There are many types of braids to choose from, including French braids, fishtail braids, Dutch braids, and waterfall braids. Braids can be worn in a variety of styles, such as a single braid down the back, multiple braids woven together, or braids wrapped around the head.

- **Loose curls or waves**: This hairstyle can be achieved with a curling iron, wand, or rollers and can be styled in different ways. Loose curls and waves offer a feminine and romantic look.

- **Sleek, straight hairstyles**: This style involves straight or straightened hair and creates a polished, smooth look that exudes elegance and sophistication. It can be worn in a variety of ways, such as parting the hair down the middle or to the side, or with a sleek and simple updo. This hairstyle is also low maintenance and easy to maintain throughout the day, making it a practical choice.

- **Side-swept hairstyles**: This style involves sweeping the hair to one side, creating an asymmetrical look that adds dimension and elegance. Side-swept hairstyles can be further enhanced with braids, curls, or hair accessories.

- **Ponytails**: Ponytails can be styled in different ways, including high, low, side, or braided, and can be dressed up or down depending on the occasion. One of the benefits of a ponytail is that it keeps the hair out of the face, making it an excellent option for dancing and other activities.

- **Shorter hairstyles**: Short haircuts range from fearless crewcuts to fun pixie cuts to sleek, sophisticated bobs and trendy lobs. Short hairstyles provide a fresh, modern, youthful look and offer many benefits, including less maintenance, faster drying times, and less hair damage from heat styling.

Remember to schedule a hair trial with your stylist before the big day so you can experiment and find the perfect style for you. Additionally, don't forget to consider any hair accessories you'll be wearing, such as a tiara or hair comb, and make sure your hairstyle works with them as well.

Makeup

Creating the perfect look for your quinceañera is essential to feeling confident and beautiful on your special day.

With so many makeup styles and techniques to choose from, it's important to consider the look you want to achieve, whether it's natural and subtle, or bold and glamorous. You will also need to factor in how it will appear in photos and videos, as the camera can accentuate certain features and wash out others.

When deciding on a makeup style, consider your personal preferences, the style of your dress, and the overall theme of your quinceañera. A natural makeup look is always a classic choice, while a glamorous look can add drama and sophistication. Decide on the vibe you're going for: do you want your look to be vintage and retro, bold and colorful, or romantic and feminine?

Doing a trial run with a makeup artist before the big day can help ensure that you get the look you want and avoid any surprises.

Bring reference photos or inspiration images to show the makeup artist what you're looking for, and be sure to communicate any preferences or concerns you may have. Be sure to take photos of the finished look to refer back to on the day of your quinceañera.

Finally, with all the dancing, photo-taking, and festivities, it's important to make sure your makeup lasts all day and is easy to retouch.

Here's an overview of some of the steps commonly found in the makeup application process and the types of products that might be used:

Skincare

Begin by cleansing your face to remove any dirt, oil, or makeup from the skin. Follow up with a moisturizer to hydrate the skin and prevent dryness. Finally, apply sunscreen to protect your skin from harmful UV rays.

Primer

Smooth on a thin layer of primer to create a smooth, even base for your foundation. This will help your makeup go on smoothly and last longer.

Foundation

Choose a foundation that matches your skin tone and apply it all over your face using a brush or sponge.

Foundation is the base of any makeup look. Think of it as your canvas and everything else you apply on top of it as your palette. It's important to choose the right foundation for your skin type, tone, coverage, and finish you desire.

There are many different types of foundation finishes available:

- **Dewy**: Provides a radiant, glowing finish that is perfect for those with dry or normal skin.

- **Matte**: Matte foundation is ideal for oily skin as it helps to control shine and gives a smooth, velvety finish.

- **Luminous**: a hybrid between dewy and matte, providing a natural-looking glow without looking too shiny.

- **Airbrush**: a popular choice for those who want a flawless finish that looks like the makeup has been airbrushed onto the skin

- **HD**: a special formulation intended to look great on camera and provide a high-definition finish that looks flawless in photos and videos.

Concealer

Dab a small amount of concealer onto any dark circles, blemishes, or areas of redness, and blend well.

Bronzer

Use a large, fluffy brush to apply bronzer to the areas of your face where the sun would naturally hit, such as your forehead, cheeks, and nose. This will add warmth and definition to your face.

Blush
Apply blush to the apples of your cheeks using a small, angled brush. Blend well for a natural-looking flush.

Highlighter
Use a small brush to apply highlighter to the high points of your face, such as your cheekbones, brow bone, and the bridge of your nose. This will add a subtle glow to your complexion.

Eye makeup
Apply eyeshadow to your lids using a brush or your fingertips. Follow up with eyeliner, applying it close to the lash line to define your eyes. Finish with a coat of mascara to make your lashes look long and full. Waterproof mascara will help prevent smudging or running, especially during emotional moments.

Makeup artists use a variety of techniques to enhance the eyes, depending on the desired look. Some popular eye makeup techniques include:

- **Cut crease**: This technique involves carving out a crease on the eyelid with a contrasting color of eyeshadow to make the eye look more defined and lifted.

- **Smokey eye**: A classic makeup technique, the smokey eye involves layering shades of eyeshadow in a gradient from light to dark, blended out for a soft, smoky effect.

- **Winged eyeliner**: Winged eyeliner involves creating a dramatic, upward flick at the outer corner of the eye with liquid or gel eyeliner.

- **Halo eye**: A lighter shade of eyeshadow is applied to the center of the eyelid, surrounded by a darker shade on the outer and inner corners of the eye.

- **Foiling**: Eyeshadow is applied wet with a damp brush, giving the eyeshadow a more intense, metallic finish.

- **Graphic eyeliner**: A bold, modern look, graphic eyeliner involves creating shapes or lines with liquid or gel eyeliner for a high-impact eye look.

- **Colored eyeliner**: Adding a pop of color to the lash line with bright or pastel eyeliner is a fun and playful way to switch up your eye makeup.

False Eyelashes and Eyelash Extensions

False eyelashes and eyelash extensions are two different ways to enhance the look of eyelashes. False eyelashes are temporary and can be applied at home using adhesive glue. They come in a variety of lengths, styles, and materials, such as synthetic or mink. They can also be removed easily at the end of the day, making them a convenient and affordable option.

Eyelash extensions are a semi-permanent solution that involves attaching individual extensions to each natural lash using a special adhesive. They typically last several weeks, with the need for touch-ups every 2-4 weeks. Eyelash extensions are a great option for those who want a longer-lasting enhancement to their lashes, without having to deal with the hassle of applying false lashes every day.

However, eyelash extensions require a bigger investment of time and money than false lashes, as they need to be applied by a professional and maintained regularly. Additionally, some people may experience irritation or allergic reactions to the adhesive used in eyelash extensions. Finally, improper removal of extensions can damage natural lashes. It's important to do your research and choose a reputable salon and experienced technician if you decide to go for eyelash extensions.

Eyebrows

Well-groomed eyebrows can make a big difference in your overall look. If you have thin or sparse eyebrows, consider filling them in with a brow pencil or powder. Use short, feathery strokes to mimic the look of natural brow hairs. For a more natural look, you can use a tinted brow gel to enhance your natural eyebrow shape.

Lips

When choosing a lip color, consider the overall look you're going for as it can have a big impact. A natural, nude lip color is perfect for a more subtle look, while a bold red or dark berry shade can add drama and glamour. To make your lip color last longer, apply a lip liner first and then fill in your lips with your chosen shade.

Powder or Setting Spray

Finally, set your makeup in place by dusting a translucent powder all over your face or using a setting spray. This will help your makeup stay put throughout the day, control shine, and give it the desired finish

Self-Care

As you get caught up in the planning process and excitement of the day, it's easy to forget to take care of yourself. However, taking the time to focus on your mental and physical health will help you look and feel your best on your special day. Consider it an investment in yourself.

Make time for activities that make you feel relaxed and happy. Whether it's going for a run, reading a book, or taking a walk in nature. Finding time to decompress and destress can have a positive impact on your overall well-being.

One way to make sure you have time for self-care is to schedule it in your calendar and then commit to it. It could be 15 minutes in the morning after you wake to do stretches in your room or go for a 30-minute walk. Set an intention and make that your time for yourself.

Here are a few things you may consider incorporating into your self-care routine:

- **Getting enough sleep**: It's recommended that teenagers get at least 8 hours of sleep each night.

- **Eating a healthy diet**: This means consuming a balanced diet that includes a variety of fruits, vegetables, whole grains, lean proteins, and healthy fats.

- **Staying hydrated**: Drinking plenty of water throughout the day can help keep you hydrated and improve overall health.

- **Exercising regularly**: Regular physical activity can help reduce stress, improve mood, and boost overall health.

- **Practicing relaxation techniques**: This can include things like meditation, deep breathing, or yoga to help reduce stress and anxiety.

- **Spending time with friends and family**: Social connections can help provide support and reduce stress.

- **Pursuing hobbies or interests**: Take time to engage in activities that bring joy or relaxation.

- **Limiting screen time**: Too much screen time can contribute to stress and anxiety. Observe what you spend time doing and how it makes you feel. It's important to take breaks and engage in other activities.

- **Seeking help when needed**: If you're struggling with your mental health or experiencing significant stress, it's important to seek help from a trusted adult or mental health professional.

Remember, self-care isn't selfish, it's necessary. Taking care of yourself will help you feel confident, happy, and ready to celebrate your quince to the fullest.

CHAPTER TWELVE

Music & Dance

A MONG THE MOST ANTICIPATED events at a quinceañera are the dances. They typically include a dance with the father and/or mother, a formal dance with the court of honor, and a fun, group dance with the damas and chambelanes. We'll explore each of these dances in detail, including tips on selecting the perfect music, choreography, and special touches to make the dances truly unforgettable.

We'll also cover the music selection for the dances and the reception. This includes hiring DJs and bands, as well as creating your own playlist. We'll explore the pros and cons of each option and provide tips on how to create a playlist that will keep your guests dancing all night long.

Dancing

At a quinceañera, three dances play a central role in the celebration: the father-daughter dance (*Baile de Papá*) and/or mother-daughter dance (*Baile de Mamá*) dance, the group waltz (*El Vals*), and the surprise dance (*El Baile Sorpresa*). These dances not only showcase the skills and elegance of the quinceañera but also her bond with her family and friends.

If you're looking to add a bit of extra flair to your quinceañera, or if you're simply unsure of how to do a particular dance, you might consider hiring a choreographer. A choreographer is a professional who is trained in creating and teaching dance routines for various events, and they can be an indispensable resource when it comes to planning the dances for your special day.

When selecting a choreographer, it's important to look for someone who has experience with the type of dance you're looking to perform, as well as someone who has a teaching style that works well with you and your group. Additionally, be sure to discuss your budget and expectations upfront to ensure that you are both on the same page before moving forward with the planning process. A good choreographer can take your dance to the next level and make it a truly memorable experience.

When selecting the music for these dances, consider the overall theme and atmosphere of your quinceañera. It's essential to choose songs that resonate with you and your family, as they will set the tone for these special moments and create lasting memories.

The Group Waltz (*El Vals*)

The waltz is one of the most important dances at a quinceañera. It is a formal and elegant dance that typically involves the quinceañera, her escort, and her court of honor. Many families choose to use a traditional waltz song or a more contemporary piece, depending on their preferences and the overall theme of the event.

The Surprise Dance (*El Baile Sorpresa*)

The surprise dance is an opportunity for the quinceañera to showcase her personality and individuality. This dance is typically choreographed and rehearsed in advance, with the quinceañera often joined by her court of honor or a group of friends.

The music for this dance can vary greatly, ranging from traditional Latin tunes to modern pop hits or a medley of songs that hold personal significance for the birthday girl. Popular dance genres for the surprise dance at a quinceañera include hip-hop, tango, cha-cha, bachata, reggaeton, salsa, merengue, and modern pop or contemporary dance styles. The choice of genre allows the birthday girl to showcase her personality and make the performance truly unique and memorable.

The Father-Daughter (*Baile de Papá*) or Mother-Daughter Dance (*Baile de Mamá*)

This is typically an emotional and heartfelt dance symbolizing the bond between the quinceañera and her father or mother. It is a special moment for both, as the father "gives away" his daughter, signifying her transition into womanhood. This dance can also be with a padrino or madrina or any parental figure.

Music for the Dances

Here are a selection of songs that are popular at quinceañeras:

Waltz Music

"Tiempo de Vals" by Chayanne
"Quinceañera" by Thalia, Paulina Rubio y Lucero
"Balada Para Adelina" by Richard Clayderman
"My Heart Will Go On" by Celine Dion
"A Thousand Years" by Christina Perri
"Blue Danube Waltz" by Johann Strauss II
"La Vie en Rose" by Edith Piaf
"Danubio Azul" by Mariachi Vargas de Tecalitlán
"Waltz of the Flowers" from *The Nutcracker* by Tchaikovsky
"Can You Feel the Love Tonight" by Elton John
"Beauty and the Beast" by Celine Dion & Peabo Bryson
"At Last" by Etta James

"Moon River" by Henry Mancini
"What a Wonderful World" by Louis Armstrong
"The Way You Look Tonight" by Frank Sinatra

Father-Daughter & Mother-Daughter Dance Songs (Spanish)
"Amor Eterno" by Juan Gabriel
"A Mi Madre Querida" by Los Bukis
"Besos de Mariposa" by Miguel Ángel Guerrero
"Chiquilla Bonita" by Los Bukis
"Chiquitita Mia" by Alvaro Torres
"Creo en Ti" by Rubén Blades
"De Niña a Mujer" by Julio Iglesias
"El Privilegio de Amar" by Mijares & Lucero
"El Reloj" by Luis Miguel
"Es Mi Niña Bonita" by Vicente Fernández (Mariachi style)
"Ese Que Me Dio La Vida" by Alejandro Sanz
"Gracias Por La Vida" by Joan Manuel Serrat
"Ha Llegado Un Ángel" by Juan Gabriel
"Hermosa Experiencia" by Banda MS
"Hija" by Abraham Velazquez
"La Mejor De Todas" by Banda El Recodo
"La Que Me Hace Llorar" by Los Tigres Del Norte
"La Última Muñeca" by Los Baron De Apodaca
"Mi Niña Bonita" by Vicente Fernandez
"No Crezcas Más" by Tercer Cielo
"Padre Nuestro" by Christine D'Clario
"Por Eso Te Amo" by Rio Roma
"Que Bonita Es Esta Vida" by Jorge Celedón
"Te Amo Mamá" by Marco Antonio Solís
"Tu Guardián" by Juanes
"Tu Sangre en mi Cuerpo" by Angela Aguilar ft. Pepe Aguilar
"Vals Del Amor" by Joan Sebastian
"Yo No Sé Mañana" by Luis Enrique

Father-Daughter & Mother-Daughter Dance Songs (English)
"Angels" by Randy Travis
"A Mother's Prayer" by Celine Dion
"Because You Loved Me" by Celine Dion
"Butterfly Kisses" by Bob Carlisle
"Cinderella" by Steven Curtis
"Daddy's Girl" by Peter Cetera
"I Hope You Dance" by Lee Ann Womack
"I'll Be There" by Jackson 5
"In My Daughter's Eyes" by Martina McBride
"Letting Go" by Suzy Bogguss
"Mom" by Garth Brooks
"Mother Like Mine" by The Band Perry
"My Baby You" by Marc Anthony
"My Girl" by The Temptations
"My Little Girl" by Tim McGraw
"My Wish" by Rascal Flatts
"Oh How The Years Go By" by Amy Grant
"Promise" by Tori Amos
"Ribbon in the Sky" by Stevie Wonder
"Slipping Through My Fingers" by ABBA
"Somebody's Hero" by Jamie O'Neal
"Stand By Me" by Prince Royce
"Unforgettable" by Nat King Cole

Surprise Dance Songs
"Aguanile" by Marc Anthony
"Bailando" by Enrique Iglesias ft. Sean Paul, Descemer Bueno, Gente De Zona
"Baby Love" by The Supremes
"Because You Loved Me" by Celine Dion
"Blessed" by Elton John

"Can't Stop the Feeling" by Justin Timberlake
"Dance Again" by Jennifer Lopez ft. Pitbull
"Dancing Queen" by Abba
"Despacito" by Luis Fonsi ft. Daddy Yankee
"Don't Stop Believin'" by Journey
"Dura" by Daddy Yankee
"Dynamite" by Taio Cruz
"El Malo" by Aventura
"Fireball" by Pitbull ft. John Ryan
"Firework" by Katy Perry
"Get The Party Started" by Pink
"Holiday" by Madonna
"Hot In Here" by Nelly
"I Hope You Dance" by Lee Ann Womack
"It's My Life" by Bon Jovi
"Just A Dream" by Nelly
"Like My Mother Does" by Lauren Alaina
"Living On A Prayer" by Bon Jovi
"Shining Star" by Earth Wind Fire
"Single Ladies" by Beyoncé
"Stand by Me" by Prince Royce
"Suavemente" by Elvis Crespo
"Uptown Funk" by Mark Ronson ft. Bruno Mars
"Vivir Mi Vida" by Marc Anthony
"Waiting for Tonight" by Jennifer Lopez

Music for the Party

In addition to the music chosen for the special dances, there is also the music for the rest of your quinceañera to consider. You can hire a DJ or a band; both choices have their own advantages. Alternatively, you can create your own playlist. Whatever you choose, the goal is to keep your guests dancing and enjoying the celebration.

If you choose a DJ or a band, it's essential to communicate your preferences, including any specific songs or genres you'd like to be included. You should also discuss the schedule of events, such as when the band or DJ should start playing, when to announce the quinceañera's entrance, and when to pause for speeches and toasts. Don't forget to coordinate with your chosen entertainer about any necessary equipment, setup times, and space requirements.

Hiring a DJ

DJs often have an extensive music library, which allows them to cater to a wide range of tastes and preferences. They can also easily adjust the playlist on the fly, ensuring that your guests remain engaged and entertained throughout the event.

DJs typically require less space and setup time compared to a live band, making them a more flexible choice for some venues. When searching for a DJ, look for one with experience in quinceañeras, as they will be familiar with the necessary traditions and music styles.

Hiring a Band

A live band can bring energy and excitement to your quinceañera, creating an unforgettable atmosphere that your guests will love. The presence of live musicians can add a touch of sophistication and elegance to your celebration.

When choosing a band, consider the type of music you want for your event, as well as the band's experience and performance style. Be sure to watch videos of their past performances or attend one of their shows to get a sense of their stage presence and musical talent. Here are some options:

- **Cover bands**: Cover bands specialize in playing popular songs from different genres and periods, by a specific artist or genre, or a mix of different styles.

- **Tribute bands**: Tribute bands are a type of cover band that specifically focuses on the music of one artist or band, like Elvis or ABBA.

- **Jazz bands:** Jazz bands typically play music from the jazz genre, which can range from swing to bebop, bossa nova to fusion. They may feature a variety of instruments, including horns, piano, bass, and drums, and range from a trio to a full orchestra.

- **Latin bands:** Latin bands specialize in playing music from Latin American countries, including mariachi, salsa, merengue, bachata, and cumbia. They may feature traditional Latin instruments, such as vihuela, guitarrón, congas, bongos, and timbales.

- **Classical music ensembles:** Classical music ensembles may include string quartets, brass quintets, or other groups of classical musicians. They typically perform music from the baroque, classical, or romantic eras.

- **Rock bands:** Rock bands typically play music from the rock genre, which can range from classic rock to punk to alternative. They may feature electric guitars, bass, drums, and vocals.

- **Funk bands:** Funk bands specialize in playing music from the funk genre, which is characterized by a rhythmic and danceable groove. They may feature horns, keyboards, bass, and drums.

- **Hip-hop:** The style and presentation of a hip-hop performance can vary widely depending on the artist, but it can be a great way to add a modern and energetic vibe to the party. Some hip-hop artists may also incorporate other genres, such as R&B or pop, into their performances.

Creating Your Own Playlist

Curating your own playlist is a great option for those who want to have control over the music played at their quinceañera while keeping costs down. By crafting your own playlist, you can hand-pick every song and ensure that each track holds special meaning or captures the desired mood for your celebration.

Song Order

One important factor to consider when creating a mood with music is the order in which the songs are played. It's a good idea to start with upbeat and energetic songs to encourage guests to get up and dance. As the night progresses, you can transition to slower and more romantic songs, creating a more intimate atmosphere for the special moments of the evening.

Genres

To choose the right music for your playlist, it is important to consider the preferences of your guests. Try to include a mix of different genres that will appeal to everyone, such as Latin music, pop, hip-hop, and electronic dance music (EDM). Additionally, you should also consider the age range of your guests and include music that will appeal to both younger and older attendees. You can include some popular songs that guests are likely to know and enjoy to keep the mood upbeat.

Tempo

Another key consideration is the tempo of the music. You want to have a good mix of fast and slow songs to keep the mood varied and interesting. Fast-paced songs will keep people dancing and energized, while slower songs provide a chance for a break and a chance to catch their breath.

Lyrics

You may want to avoid music that has offensive or inappropriate lyrics, as this can bring down the mood of the party and make guests uncomfortable. Take the time to review the lyrics of each song before adding it to your playlist, or ask for input from family and friends.

Overall, creating your own playlist can be a great way to keep the music at your quinceañera in line with your personal preferences and those of your guests. With some careful consideration and planning, you can create a playlist that will keep the party going all night long.

CHAPTER THIRTEEN

Speeches & Toasts

Y OUR SPEECH PROVIDES AN opportunity for you to express your gratitude to your family and friends who have supported you throughout your life. The toasts from your loved ones allow guests to share their love and admiration for you, creating meaningful connections and a moving experience for all involved. Both serve as a moment of resonance and community, bringing everyone together to celebrate this special milestone in your life.

Speech Length

Speeches and toasts are typically given during the reception. You can schedule a block for the toasts, or they can also take place between courses or during dessert. Be mindful of the length of your speech; aim for 2-5 minutes, as a long speech can lose the audience's attention.

Coordinate with the event planner or MC to ensure speeches and toasts are scheduled appropriately into the program and don't disrupt the flow of the celebration. You should also be prepared for and welcome some spontaneous toasts as well.

Who Gives Toasts

Traditionally, the quinceañera's parents, padrinos, madrinas, and close family members give toasts. However, it's also common for friends or other special individuals in the quinceañera's life to share a few words.

Preparing a Toast to the Quinceañera

Take time to reflect on your relationship with the quinceañera and any special memories or moments that stand out. Consider what you want to convey in your speech – whether it's sharing a funny anecdote, offering words of wisdom, or expressing your love and support. Write down your thoughts and practice your toast to ensure it flows smoothly and captures the emotions you want to convey.

Tips for Delivering a Speech

Here are some tips for giving a speech:

- **Be prepared**: Practice your speech multiple times and be familiar with your material.

- **Use body language**: Maintain good posture, make eye contact, and use hand gestures to emphasize your points.

- **Speak clearly**: Speak loudly and clearly, and avoid mumbling or rushing through your words.

- **Be authentic**: Be yourself and speak from the heart. Your passion and enthusiasm will help engage your audience.

Dealing with Nerves

If the thought of standing in front of a crowd and delivering a speech ties your stomach up in knots, you're in good company! Studies show that up to 75% of people have a fear of public speaking. However, with the right mindset and preparation, most people can overcome their nerves. In fact, public speaking is an important skill that can help you academically, professionally, and in many areas of your life, and your quinceañera is a wonderful opportunity to develop that muscle.

Performers like actors, musicians, and athletes often experience performance anxiety before going on stage or in competition. Many have learned strategies to manage those feelings and still deliver a good performance. Here are some practical tips and techniques performers use that can help you deliver a successful speech:

- **Rehearse**: Ensure that you have rehearsed your performance well in advance and feel confident in your abilities.

- **Breathing exercises**: Taking deep breaths can help you calm down and reduce anxiety. Practice inhaling slowly through your nose and exhaling slowly through your mouth.

- **Visualization**: Imagine yourself performing well and getting positive feedback from the audience. Visualize yourself feeling confident and relaxed on stage.

- **Positive self-talk**: Use positive affirmations to boost your confidence. Tell yourself that you are capable of performing well and that you have prepared for this moment.

- **Focus on the present moment**: Don't worry about what might happen or what went wrong in the past. Instead, focus on the present moment and give your full attention to your performance.

- **Physical activity**: Engage in physical activity such as stretching, yoga, or exercise to help reduce stress and anxiety.

- **Connect with your audience**: Try to establish a connection with your audience, whether it's through eye contact, smiling, or engaging with them in other ways. This can help you feel more comfortable and confident on stage.

- **Warm-up exercises**: Doing warm-up exercises can help reduce tension and improve your performance.

- **Stay hydrated**: Make sure you drink enough water and also have water nearby in case your mouth and throat are dry.

- **Get enough rest**: Being well-rested can help you feel more alert, relaxed, and focused.

- **Don't be too hard on yourself**: Remember that everyone makes mistakes and that it's okay to make mistakes.

Sample Speeches and Toasts

When writing your speech, write from your heart. The more authentic you are, the easier it will be. Use short, conversational sentences, and make sure it has a clear structure: a beginning, middle, and an end.

Here are some examples of speeches and toasts that you can use as a reference for writing your own:

QUINCEAÑERA'S SPEECH:

Thank you all for being here to celebrate this wonderful day with me. As I stand before you, I feel a mix of emotions – excitement, gratitude, and even a bit of nervousness. Today, I am no longer a little girl, but a young woman stepping into a new chapter of my life.

I want to begin by thanking my parents for their unwavering love and support. Mom and Dad, you've taught me the importance of kindness, compassion, and perseverance. You've shown me what it means to be strong and resilient. I am who I am today because of your guidance and love, and I am forever grateful.

To my siblings and cousins, thank you for being my confidants, partners in crime, and lifelong friends. Our memories together are something I will always cherish.

To my grandparents, thank you for your wisdom and the rich heritage you've passed down to us. I am proud to be part of this beautiful family and to continue the legacy you have created.

To my friends, thank you for the laughter, the support, and the countless memories we've shared. You've been my rock, my support system, and my shoulders to lean on. I am grateful for each and every one of you.

As I embark on this new chapter, I'm reminded of the people, values, and traditions that have shaped me into the young woman I am today. This quinceañera is not just a celebration of my fifteenth birthday, but a celebration of my heritage, my family, and the love that surrounds me.

I am truly blessed to have all of you here today, sharing this special moment with me. I hope that tonight is a night we can all remember fondly for years to come. So, let's dance, laugh, and make memories together as we celebrate this milestone in my life. Thank you so much for being here. It means so much to me. I love you all!

Shorter toast from a family member, madrina, padrino, or friend:

I'd like to propose a toast to our beautiful quinceañera, [Name]. As we gather here to celebrate this joyous occasion, we're filled with love and pride. [Name], we've watched you blossom into a remarkable young woman. I know you have a brilliant future ahead of you and I wish you nothing but love, happiness, and success on the way. I'm so proud to be your [Relationship to Quinceañera]."

Longer toast from a parent, madrina, or padrino:

As your [Relationship to Quinceañera], it is my honor to share a few words on this special occasion.

I remember the day you were born, the first time I held you in my arms, and the moments we've shared over the years. Watching you grow into the beautiful young woman you are today has been a joy and a privilege.

You have always been driven and passionate, with a heart of gold and an unwavering commitment to your goals. From excelling in academics to shining on the dance floor, you have amazed me time and time again with your talents and achievements.

But beyond your accomplishments, what impresses me most about you is your kindness and compassion toward others. You make everyone feel loved, and I know that this quality will take you far in life.

Today, as you celebrate your quinceañera, I want you to know that I am so proud of the person you have become and excited for all the incredible things you will achieve in the future. May this day be filled with love, laughter, and memories that will last a lifetime.

Te quiero mucho Mija!

Chapter Fourteen

Document & Share

I N THIS CHAPTER, WE'LL explore the different ways you can document and share your quinceañera, ensuring that your memories are captured and cherished in a format that will bring you joy and last for years to come.

We'll look at hiring a photographer and/or videographer for your quince. We'll discuss budgets, reviewing contracts, and creating shot lists. We'll also explore the differences between photography and video, and the advantages of each so that you can decide what is best for you. Finally, we'll look at the process of creating a website, and discuss the pros and cons of sharing via social media, privacy, and safety.

Photography and Video

One of the most important decisions you'll make when planning your quinceañera is hiring a photographer and/or videographer to capture your special day. Both offer unique ways to preserve your memories, but they differ in some key ways. A photographer captures still images that can be printed and displayed in albums, frames, or canvases, while a videographer captures moving images that tell the story of your day in a more cinematic way.

When considering which to hire, think about what's most important to you. Do you want to see still images that you can easily share with family and friends or display in your home? Or do you want a more immersive experience that captures the energy and emotions of your day and moments over time? Hiring both a photographer and a videographer is an option if you want the best of both worlds.

Photos are physical keepsakes that you can display in your home or use to create albums for yourself and loved ones. A professional video will capture the parts of your quinceañera that go beyond a snapshot in time with visuals, sound, and motion, and will do so in a way that phone footage will not. You will be able to rewatch key moments from your quinceañera again, like the ceremony, dances, and toasts. You will also be able to capture people in motion, hear what they said, and how they sounded.

Here are some tips to help you choose the right photographer or videographer for your quinceañera:

Set a budget
Before you start looking for a photographer/videographer, set a budget for photography services. This will help you narrow down your options and ensure that you're not overspending.

Portfolio
The best way to see if a photographer/videographer's style matches your vision is to look at their portfolio. Check their website or social media pages to see their previous work. This will give you a good idea of their style and creativity.

Experience
Check if the photographer/videographer has experience shooting quinceañeras specifically, as well as their overall experience and

background in photography. It doesn't have to be a dealbreaker if they haven't shot a lot of quinceañeras, but it always helps.

Reviews and recommendations
Look for reviews and recommendations from other clients and ask for referrals from the photographer/videographer.

Meet in person
Once you've shortlisted a few photographers/videographers, arrange a meeting with them in person. This will allow you to ask any questions you may have and see if you feel comfortable working with them. You'll also be able to discuss any specific shots or styles that you want to be included in your photos.

References
It's always a good idea to ask for references. Speak to their previous clients and ask them about their experience with the photographer. Were they happy with the photos? Was the photographer easy to work with? Did they deliver on time?

Availability
Make sure the photographer/videographer is available on your chosen date and ask about their schedule for the day.

Equipment
Ask the photographer/videographer what equipment they use. They should have professional-grade cameras and lenses, and backup equipment in case something goes wrong. You want to ensure that they have everything they need to capture your special day.

Shot List
A shot list is a helpful tool for both you and your photographer or videographer. It outlines the specific moments and shots you want

to be captured on your special day. The shot list is a detailed break-down of the key events, important people, and essential moments you want to have captured in your photographs or video. Creating a shot list can help ensure that your photographer or videographer can capture all the moments that are most important to you and that you will have a beautiful and comprehensive record of your quinceañera.

To create a shot list, start by thinking about the most important moments of the day. This might include the ceremony, the reception, the surprise dance, and family portraits. Then, break each of these moments down into specific shots or groupings that you want to have captured. For example, during the ceremony, you might want shots of the entrance, the blessing, and the crowning.

It's important to communicate your shot list to your photographer or videographer well in advance of the event, so they can plan accordingly and make sure they have the necessary equipment and time to capture everything on your list. You can also review the shot list with your photographer or videographer on the day of the event to ensure that everyone is on the same page.

While a shot list is helpful, it's also important to be flexible and open to capturing spontaneous moments that may arise throughout the day. Your photographer or videographer may have their own ideas and creative suggestions that can make your memories even more special.

Editing
Ask about the photographer/videographer's editing process. Photographers often offer retouching or other enhancements to the photos. Videographers may not edit the video themselves, but hire video editors who have special skills and know how to use professional video editing software, to make videos more cinematic.

Image delivery
Ask about the timeline for receiving your photos/videos and

whether you will have access to digital files or prints. Videos may come in different formats and media and you want to be clear about what the final output will be.

Albums and prints
If you want a physical album or prints, ask about the options and prices. Consider making your own album with a quality lab if you prefer more control over the design and lower costs.

Photography Packages
Most event photographers will offer a range of packages to choose from, with varying levels of coverage and products included. Packages may include a set number of hours of coverage, a certain number of edited images, and additional options such as prints, albums, or digital files. It's important to review each package and understand exactly what is included, as well as any additional fees for things like travel or extra time.

For example, one photographer may offer a basic package with 6 hours of coverage and a certain number of edited photos, while another may offer a premium package with unlimited coverage, multiple photographers, and an album included. Be sure to ask about additional charges for services such as extra editing or travel expenses.

When discussing packages with your photographer, consider what you want to do with your photos after the event. Do you want a digital gallery to share with friends and family or do you want physical prints or an album? Many photographers offer album options, and it's important to understand what's included in the package.

Videography Packages
Videography packages may include a basic package that covers the ceremony and highlights of the reception, while more comprehensive packages may include additional coverage such as the

pre-ceremony preparation, full coverage of the reception, and a longer, edited video.

Videos are typically provided as DVDs, Blu-rays, or USB drives. Some might include a highlight reel that can be accessed via YouTube or Vimeo. Most packages will include a full-length, edited feature video, a highlight reel, and raw footage. You may also have the option to make a round of edits to your video. Extras like drone footage, Super 8 film, or additional DVDs or USB drives are usually available for an additional fee.

Pricing

Some photographers may charge a flat fee for their services, while others may charge an hourly rate or a per-image rate. The per-image rate may be based on the number of edited images provided or the total number of images taken during the event.

Additionally, some photographers may require a deposit or retainer fee to reserve your date and ensure their availability. This fee is typically non-refundable and may be applied toward your final payment.

Videographers may charge an hourly rate, where the videographer charges a set amount per hour of filming or editing. It's more common, however, to charge by project or package rate, such as filming the entire quinceañera event and creating a highlight reel.

Services such as video editing, may be charged separately. The final price will also depend on factors such as the length of the final video, the number of cameras used, the complexity of the project, and any additional equipment or crew needed. It's important to discuss all of these details with the videographer and get a clear understanding of their pricing structure before hiring them for the job.

Cancellation Policy

Ask about the photographer's cancellation policy and make sure it's stated in the contract.

Rights and Restrictions
Ask about any restrictions the photographer may have on using the photos for personal or commercial use.

Contract
Once you've chosen a photographer, make sure you sign a contract that outlines all the details of the service. This should include:

• Price
• Package options
• Date and time of the shoot
• Scope of the service
• Cancellation policy
• Number of hours of coverage
• Number of photographers/videographers
• Editing and proofing
• The delivery date of the photos/videos
• Albums
• Rights to the photos
• Additional fees or requirements

Creating Your Own Album
Creating your own photo albums can be a great option for those looking to save money or who have specific preferences in mind for their album design. While professional photographers and videographers often offer high-quality albums that are specifically tailored to the style of the event, making your own album can be a fun and creative way to personalize the memories of your special day.

There are a variety of online printing services available, such as Shutterfly, Snapfish, and Mixbook, that allow you to create your own custom photo albums. While these services may be more affordable than a professional album, it's important to keep in mind that the quality of the final product may not be on par with what a professional photographer can provide.

It's important to note that creating your own album will require some effort and time investment on your part. You'll need to spend time selecting and uploading your photos, and then designing the album to your liking. However, the end result can be a beautiful and personalized album that captures the memories of your special day in a unique and meaningful way.

If you choose to create your own album, it's recommended that you use a high-quality printing service and pay close attention to the design and layout of the album. A well-designed and thought-fully curated album can be just as meaningful and valuable as a professionally designed one.

Creating a Website

Making a website for your quinceañera can be a great way to share your special day. It can also serve as a centralized place for all your event-related information. There are many website-building platforms you can use to create a beautiful and informative website that serves as a memento of your celebration. There are also free and paid options, so be sure to review the terms and conditions of each.

This section will give you an overview of creating a website for your quinceañera:

Choose a Platform

Select a website-building platform that suits your needs and skill level. Platforms like Wix, Squarespace, WordPress, and Weebly offer templates and tools to make the process of building a website easier, even for those without web design experience.

Be sure to use a reputable web hosting service that provides secure socket layer (SSL) encryption and protection against malware and other online threats. Additionally, use strong passwords and keep them private. Using a password manager like LastPass, 1Password, or Bitwarden is recommended. You may also want to consider limiting access to your website by requiring a password for visitors or keeping it private and sharing the link only with those you trust. Finally, make sure to keep your website up-to-date with the latest security patches and updates to help prevent any potential security breaches.

Pick a Domain Name and Hosting Plan

Choose a memorable and unique domain name that reflects the essence of your quinceañera. This will serve as your website's address on the internet. Most website-building platforms offer domain registration and hosting plans as part of their services. Ensure that you choose a hosting plan that meets your needs in terms of storage, bandwidth, and cost.

Select a Template and Design

Browse through the available templates on your chosen platform and pick one that aligns with the theme and aesthetic of your quinceañera. Customize the template by choosing colors, fonts, and images that represent your style and the spirit of the celebration. Keep your design clean and simple, ensuring that the website is easy to navigate and visually appealing.

Create Essential Pages

Your quinceañera website should have several essential pages, including:

- **Home**: This is the first page visitors will see when they access your website. Include a welcome message, a beautiful photo, and a brief introduction to your quinceañera.

- **About**: Share your story and the significance of your quinceañera. You can also include information about your family and the traditions that will be part of your celebration.

- **Event Details**: Provide all the necessary information about the event, such as date, time, venue, dress code, and any special instructions for guests.

- **RSVP**: Create an easy-to-use RSVP form for guests to confirm their attendance and provide any additional information, such as dietary restrictions or song requests.

- **Gallery**: Showcase photos and videos from your quinceañera, including pre-event photoshoots, the ceremony, and the reception.

Add Social Media Integration

Integrate your social media accounts to encourage guests to share photos and messages about your quinceañera. Create a unique hashtag for your event to make it easy for everyone to find and contribute to the online conversation.

Test and Launch

Before launching your website, test it on various devices and browsers to ensure that it displays correctly and functions smoothly. Once you're satisfied with your website, share the link with your guests through invitations, social media, or email.

Social Media

Social media can be a useful tool to share updates and information about your quinceañera with friends and family. From announcing the date and theme to sharing photos and videos of the festivities, social media can help you keep everyone in the loop.

When it comes to using social media for your quinceañera, timing is important. You may want to create a dedicated Instagram account or Facebook page for your event and start posting updates and sneak peeks several months before the big day. This can build anticipation and excitement among your guests.

When posting, make sure to use appropriate hashtags to make it easier for others to find and follow your event. You may also want to consider creating a custom hashtag specific to your quinceañera.

It's important to remember that not all of your guests may be active on social media, so it's still a good idea to send out traditional invitations and updates through email or other means as well.

Finally, as a rule of thumb, it's a good idea to set your account to private and only accept friend requests from those you know personally.

Privacy and Security
While social media can be a great way to communicate, document, and share your quinceañera, it's important to be mindful of what you share. While it may be tempting to share everything about your quinceañera, some things are best kept private.

Please take the time to understand the implications of social media and how to use it safely and responsibly, and always prioritize the privacy and security of yourself and your guests.

Be sure to familiarize yourself with privacy settings on your preferred social media platforms and use them to control who can see your posts and photos. It's also important to understand that privacy settings are not foolproof. Even if you have set your account to private, someone could still take a screenshot of your post and share it publicly. So, it's important to think carefully about what you post and consider the potential consequences.

Avoid publicly sharing personal information, like your address or phone number, and think twice about posting photos or videos that could be used to identify your location particularly before and during the event.

Use caution before sharing anything that could be embarrassing or potentially damaging to yourself or others. Remember that anything you post online can be seen by anyone, including current or future employers, college admissions officers, and even strangers.

It's also important to consider the privacy and security of your guests. Some guests may not want their photos or personal information shared on social media. Always ask for their permission before posting a photo or tagging them in a post. Consider creating a private group or event page where only guests can see and share photos.

One aspect of becoming a young adult is to be mindful of your digital footprint and to prioritize your personal safety and mental well-being, as well as others. By being proactive and making informed choices about what, when, and how you share it, you can enjoy the benefits of social media while minimizing the risks. Remember, you're in control of your online presence, so think before you post!

Chapter Fifteen

Post-Event Tasks & Reflections

Congratulations, you did it! Your big day was a huge success! High fives all around for a job well done! But before you ride off toward 16, there are some post-event tasks you may need to attend to in the days and weeks ahead to ensure that your quinceañera experience is wrapped up in a tidy bow and brought to a close.

Thank you notes

One of the most important tasks is to send thank-you notes to your guests. It's always a good idea to show your appreciation for their presence, gifts, and contributions to your special day. You can go old school and send handwritten notes, or you can go paperless and send e-cards or messages via social media or email.

Photography & videography

If you hired a photographer or videographer, be sure to review their work and submit your feedback promptly.

You may also want to share your photos and videos with your

guests. There are many options including sending a thank-you card with images from your quinceañera, printed albums, or a private album on a photo-sharing website or social media platform. As always, make sure to ask for permission from your guests before sharing any photos publicly on social media.

If you created a website, that is also a good place to post a thank you to your guests, along with an edited selection of photos and videos of the day.

Rentals, storage, & payments

Remember to return any rentals, borrowed, or unused items, settle outstanding bills or payments, and put into safe storage your dress and any keepsakes or mementos from your quinceañera that you want to preserve.

Written documentation & journaling

Now that you've been through the entire process you may have insights you want to capture and share. You can document the experience by writing captions for your photos on social media, in a scrapbook, or in a photo album. You can also write voiceovers for your videos.

It's a good idea to write down your thoughts and reflections while your memories are still fresh. Your future self will thank you for taking the time to do it. There are many methods you can use to document your thoughts and feelings. Journaling is a great way to preserve your memories and reflect on your experiences. You may even choose to keep a journal throughout the process of planning your quinceañera.

Choose the method you want to use, whether it's a pen-and-paper journal or a digital journaling app. Write down your reflections and thoughts from the day while those memories are still top-of-mind. A journal will allow you to revisit the day in the years to come and recall what you were thinking and doing during all those special moments.

Here are some journal question prompts to get you started:

- What was the theme of your quinceañera and why did you choose it?

- What were some of your favorite parts of the quinceañera celebration?

- What did you learn about yourself during the planning process?

- What were some challenges you faced during the planning process, and how did you overcome them?

- Who were the most important people who helped you plan and execute the quinceañera, and why?

- How did you feel during the quinceañera ceremony?

- What were the most memorable moments of the day?

- What was the biggest surprise of the day?

- What did you learn about your family and friends during the process?

- How did you feel during the surprise dance?

- What were the best gifts you received?

- What are some things you want to remember about the day?

- What are some of your favorite quotes from the day?

- What did you say during your speech?

- What did people say during their toasts?

- Were there any other quotes that you wanted to capture?

- What would you tell your younger self now that you've been through the process?

- What would you tell a girl who is about to embark on planning her quinceañera?

- What are some things you would do differently if you were to plan another quinceañera?

- How do you feel now that the quinceañera is over?

- What are some of the most valuable lessons you learned?

CHAPTER SIXTEEN

The Next Chapter

P LEASE TAKE A MOMENT to appreciate the incredible journey you've been on. Your quinceañera has provided you with an opportunity to learn and grow in ways that you may never have thought possible. The experience has equipped you with valuable life skills in decision-making, budgeting, time management, and leadership that will serve you well in your next chapter, and the chapters after that.

You've honed your communication skills, gotten organized, and learned how to manage your mindset. You've practiced the art of negotiation and learned to balance different perspectives while knowing when to be assertive and decisive. The confidence and determination you gained from this experience will help you achieve your goals, whether you're pursuing an education, career, new interests, responsibilities, or pursuits.

Finally, don't forget the love and support you received from your family and friends throughout this entire process. They were there to help you every step of the way and will continue to be a source of encouragement and guidance in the future. And now you, with your experience and knowledge, can perhaps be that for someone else, a mentor.

So, take a deep breath, smile, and celebrate the "new you" you've become through this journey.

Your quinceañera has given you lasting memories and an enduring sense of self — and you looked absolutely stunning doing it! As you step into the next chapter of your life, know that you are capable, empowered, and ready to take on the world. Use this experience to give you the confidence to chase your dreams and make a difference. Keep shining, sis — you've got this!

About the Author

Isa Martinez is an event planner and consultant with a wealth of experience in crafting exceptional celebrations. After a successful career as an executive and business coach for some of the world's biggest brands where she honed her skills in leadership, management, and creative problem-solving, she followed her passion to bring happiness to people through expertly-planned and executed events and experiences.

MORE QUINCEAÑERA BOOKS FROM OH HAPPY DAY PRESS

Guest Books

The Essential Quinceañera Planner (Workbook)

Quinceañera Photo Album and Memory Book

If you found this book helpful, please consider leaving a review on Amazon or the retailer you bought it from. Thank you!

Made in the USA
Columbia, SC
10 June 2024

b919e615-fd07-4712-acc9-fab8367dc3baR01